Wolf Boy

Wolf Boy

A Case of Mistaken Identity

By Michele Rae Eich

VMI Publishers
Sisters, Oregon

Wolf Boy: A Case of Mistaken Identity
© 2009 by Michele Rae Eich
All rights reserved. Published 2009.

Published by
VMI Publishers
Sisters, Oregon
www.vmipublishers.com

ISBN: 1-933204-93-1
ISBN 13: 978-1-933204-93-2
Library of Congress Control Number: 2009924123

Printed in the USA.

Cover design by Juanita Dix

TABLE OF CONTENTS

Chapter 1   Steven 1

Chapter 2   Identity Theft 15

Chapter 3   Split Personality? 25

Chapter 4   Horse and Cart 37

Chapter 5   Behavior Mod 101 51

Chapter 6   Enemy Territory 59

Chapter 7   Victory 71

Chapter 8   Sinful Nature 81

Chapter 9   Rules and Regulations 89

Chapter 10   True Freedom 103

Chapter 11   Reflections 113

About the Author 121

Identity Verses 123

Questions for Discussion 127

DEDICATION

I dedicate this book to my Lord and Savior, Jesus Christ
Who has given me new and abundant life in Him;
and to my husband, Lynn.
Without his support and encouragement,
it never would have been written.

"And I will restore to you the years that the
locust hath eaten"—Joel 2:25 (ASV)

INTRODUCTION

Sin, repent, succeed, fail. Sin, repent, succeed, fail. This is a picture of the lives of many people today. How can they get off of the treadmill going nowhere? Is there a better way?

In the book *Wolf Boy: A Case of Mistaken Identity*, author Michele Rae Eich weaves a tale of a baby boy named Steven who mysteriously disappears without a trace during his family's vacation. When he is found years later, the boy does not know who or what he is. Attempts to bring him back to the world of humans fail miserably. His parents try everything in their power to reach their son to no avail. Will they discover the key which could unlock the door to Steven's world of darkness and deception?

Many people see a need for improvement in their lives. However, they simply do not know how to experience true change that lasts. Instead they find themselves on the treadmill of self-effort which only leads to failure and frustration. After exerting a lot of energy and still going nowhere, many individuals simply quit trying and give up all together.

Actions do not define who a person is, but who a person is will influence his actions. People tend to focus on behavior instead of the root issue which causes it. Typically, the problem is a case of mistaken identity. When people know who they are and to whom they belong, then their actions will line up with those truths. Real change works its way from the inside out, and it begins with the heart. Who is the only one who can change the heart? God. Once He does, then what? The answer moves people forward into their destinies. No more treadmill!

Victory is possible, and this book uses the story of a very confused little boy to show people how to attain it. *Wolf Boy* is a thought-provoking story which will get its readers thinking in new ways as they journey toward inner discovery. It reveals the one key element in recognizing a person's real identity. This key will unlock the door to an amazing adventure and a future filled with freedom, peace, and joy.

Chapter 1

STEVEN

K evin and Anna Graham had it all. They were young and in love and the proud parents of a beautiful, healthy and energetic little boy named Steven. As a third anniversary celebration, they decided to take their ninth-month-old on a camping trip to the mountains near their home in Colorado Springs. This was the Grahams' first vacation since his birth, and Kevin and Anna decided that a few days in the spring mountain air would be refreshing for everyone. Starry nights, campfires and breathtaking views would provide a time of relaxation for the entire family.

The joy of vacation and the relaxed pace of the trip soon turned to tragedy. The young parents awoke on a crisp, cool morning to discover that their son was gone. The panic rose within them immediately as they searched frantically around the campsite, looking for their little boy. There was no sign of him anywhere. Could he have crawled away? Had he been kidnapped? With each passing moment, terror enveloped them as they clung to the hope of finding their baby.

Kevin called 911, and Sheriff Demott was on the scene within minutes. He was a seasoned investigator and knew the terrain better than anyone. The sheriff immediately discovered some wolf tracks near the tent and feared the worst although he kept this first hunch to himself. He called in reinforcements and immediately set up a search party to comb the woods thoroughly. Steven's parents also searched desperately for their little boy and prayed for a miracle.

The search continued for several days, and the media brought the nation's attention to the story. Hundreds of people volunteered to help, but no one found the little boy. After a week, they officially called off the search. Sheriff Demott delivered the devastating news. "I'm so sorry. We did everything we could."

Steven was presumed dead, but his parents did not want to give up. They continued to search on their own to no avail. Finally, they went home in utter exhaustion and monumental grief. Their precious angel was gone without a trace.

Unbeknownst to Kevin and Anna, a female wolf had crept into their tent in the middle of the night to drag Steven away. Since she had recently lost her cubs to poachers, she was desperate to replace them. The wolf took Steven to her den which lay beneath the earth near a labyrinth of tunnels. Rescue workers had stood above the very spot where Steven cried for his mother. However, they could not hear the baby's muffled whimpers since he was held captive so far underground.

Days turned into weeks, and months turned into years. The tragedy impacted the entire community profoundly. People kept their children close for years to come. Kevin and Anna moved away from the area to try to distance themselves from daily reminders of their unfathomable grief. They tried to overcome their loss, but they never forgot the little boy with curly hair, brown eyes, and a dimple on his chin. Because they did not know what had happened to their baby, the Grahams had no closure, and thoughts of their missing son tortured them for years.

Sheriff Demott eventually retired but was plagued with questions about the mysterious disappearance of Steven. Every law enforcement official hates to see a case remain unsolved. This one tore at his heart more than others as pictures of Steven had reminded him of his own grandson. He could not let it go.

Five years had passed since the disappearance of Kevin and Anna's pride and joy. They had two more children, a boy and a girl, and they tried to put the nightmare behind them. Sheriff Demott also tried to move on, but something incredible happened that brought the story back to his mind, and once again, he gave it his full attention.

He was having his morning coffee at a local restaurant where people in the small town learned about the news, weather and other important tidbits of information. He overheard a group of hunters talking about their morning hunt. The former sheriff guessed they were not from the area since he knew all of the locals.

"I don't know what it was either, but I know it wasn't a wolf," said one.

"I didn't see anything except for your pale face. You looked like you saw a ghost," replied his friend.

"It almost looked human, but how could it have been?" added the third man.

Sheriff Demott walked over to the table and asked the men what they were talking about. They told him that they had seen some wolves feeding on a deer carcass, but one of them looked strange and almost human.

"If it was a human—and I'm not saying it was—about how old would you guess him to be?" asked the sheriff.

"Oh, I don't know, maybe four. He wasn't very big, and he ran away with the wolves once he saw us. It was the strangest thing I've every seen in all my years in the woods."

"Could you tell me where you saw this boy ... I mean creature? I'd like to check it out," said the sheriff. He thought to himself, *Could it be? Could it possibly be?*

Sheriff Demott immediately called his veterinarian friend, Tom Welker, and told him to bring a dart gun with sedatives and some smoke sticks in case they had to force animals out of a hole. The vet was a good friend of the sheriff and knew better than to ask him any questions. They headed to the spot the hunters described.

After searching the area for nearly two hours, they came upon what appeared to be a tunnel, possibly leading to a wolf den. The sheriff signaled to Tom to throw the sticks into the den. Once he did that, they waited for the fury that was to be released. Three wolves immediately came boiling out of the den. When they saw the men, they quickly darted away. A few minutes later another creature crept out of the den, but it was no wolf. It began to scurry away. Sheriff Demott yelled to Tom, "Shoot him now!"

The speechless vet shot the creature with the dart gun, and as it tried to crawl away, it tumbled into the leaves and collapsed.

The sheriff walked over to the creature to discover that his hunch had been correct. Even though he had anticipated finding the boy, he could scarcely believe his eyes. He was human all right, but he was covered with dirt and smelled horrid. His hair was matted, and his nails were sharp and curled. He bent down to touch his little face. "Hello, Steven."

The men loaded the limp little boy into their vehicle and drove him to the nearest hospital. Once the hospital personnel got him cleaned up, they strapped him to the bed upon the sheriff's recommendation. "When he wakes up, he is going to be like a wild animal who will be very angry. You might want to keep him sedated as long as possible," he suggested. The sheriff spoke briefly to the doctor and excused himself. "I have an important phone call to make."

Calling Kevin and Anna Graham after all of these years filled the sheriff with conflicting emotions. He thought he'd seen it all during his thirty-year career on the force, but the compassion that he felt for this couple overwhelmed him. Somehow this little family had softened his old calloused heart. He never forgot the look on their faces when he ended the search for their son. It was time to solve this mystery, but what were they going to have to face next?

"Hello, Mrs. Graham? This is Sheriff Demott. How are you, M'am?"

Anna had not heard the man's voice in years. It immediately tore open the wound that had never really healed within her heart. She had spoken to the sheriff a few times in the months after Steven's mysterious disappearance. They had been given some leads that were dead ends which only got their hopes up for nothing. "Yes, Sheriff, how are you?"

"I'm fine. Listen, I have some news for you. Are you sitting down? I believe that we've found your son, Steven."

Immediately Anna's heart sank. Her only thought was that they had discovered his tiny bones somewhere, and he could finally have a proper burial. "I, um, Sheriff ... I don't ... where is he?" she whispered.

"He is at Mercy Hospital. Anna, he's alive." He then heard a loud thump as she hit the floor.

Anna and Kevin put their two children in the van and headed to the hospital, which was two hours away. The drive seemed endless, and they had so many thoughts running through their minds. They finally pulled up to the emergency room doors, and Anna sprinted inside as Kevin cared for the two younger children. Sheriff Demott met Anna at the door and hugged her. He knew that he would have to prepare the woman for the sight she was about to see. "Where is he? Where is our son?"

"Now wait just a minute, Mrs. Graham. There are a few things you need to know before you go in there."

"Wait? I've been waiting to hold him for five years! I want to see him now!"

"I understand. He has been heavily sedated. The doctors checked him over, and he seems fine. Physically he is very healthy, but ...."

"OK, then, what is the problem?"

"Mrs. Graham, we found Steven in a wolf den. When he disappeared, I had seen some wolf tracks around your campsite. I feared that he had been eaten by wolves, but it looks like they took him in. They have raised him for the past five years. For all practical purposes, he is a wild animal. If he were to wake up right now, he would go crazy."

His words swirled around Anna's head, and she could barely register them. By then her husband had arrived, and he too wanted to see his son.

"I will keep a close eye on these youngsters while you two go visit your boy."

The trembling parents walked into the room. The little boy was hooked up to tubes and monitors. His brown hair was long and curly. Anna reached down and touched the dimple on his chin. She knew he was her son. Both parents collapsed on top of their boy, and uncontrollable sobs wracked their bodies. Their prayers had been answered. Steven was alive, and they had been reunited with their precious little boy after all these years.

Joy soon turned to sorrow as they met with doctors to discuss his prognosis. "Mr. and Mrs. Graham, I am Dr. Olson, and I have been monitoring your son. We have him sedated, and when the medicine wears off, he will become very agitated. I am not sure that you want to take him home at this point, although physically he seems fine. My recommendation is to have him hospitalized for a time until he can be better evaluated by a team of—"

"No! I am taking him home with me. I have been waiting to have him for years, and he needs to be with his family. Release him to us immediately!" insisted Anna.

"Mrs. Graham, I don't think you understand the severity—"

"I will not hear another word of it. You are not going to keep my son here. He's going home!" she cried.

"Mr. and Mrs. Graham," Dr. Olson began, "your son could provide valuable information for scientists. A find like this is so rare that—"

"My son is not going to be part of a science experiment in some laboratory. Release him to us immediately!" demanded Kevin.

The following day, Sheriff Demott helped the Grahams take Steven home. They put him in the back of a squad car for the two-hour drive, but he was still heavily medicated. The doctors recommended that he be given sedatives periodically to help him deal with the trauma he would surely face as he reentered the world of humans.

"For all practical purposes, you are bringing a wild animal, a wolf, into your home. I want you to understand that," Dr. Olson had warned him that morning.

"Thank you for all you've done, Doctor. I'm sure that Steven will be fine," replied Kevin.

They brought Steven home, where they were surprised by friends and family who had heard the good news and wanted to celebrate. These were people who had spent days looking for the little boy and had been heartbroken at his disappearance. Everyone wanted just a glimpse of the little boy.

Kevin carried Steven into the house, and the sedatives were beginning to wear off. He started to squirm and growl, so his father took him to the back bedroom and gave him another injection. "I know you all mean well, but we need some time to get Steven familiar with his new surroundings. Thank you for coming, but we are going to need some privacy at this time," said Kevin. People began to file out, wondering what had really happened to Steven.

Life in the Graham household soon became very challenging. Steven needed round-the-clock care and supervision. Anna and Kevin did not want to keep their son in a drug-induced coma, but when he was awake, he behaved erratically. The two younger children were afraid of their older brother and kept their distance.

Steven would crawl on all fours and try to escape from the house. He would snarl and show his teeth to his parents as a low guttural growl came from him. It disturbed Anna so much that she could barely stand it. When Steven slept, they could approach him, but when he was fully awake, he wanted to seclude himself completely.

After a few days, the parents decided that it was time to get some help for their son. They consulted a child psychiatrist who came to their home to view the boy firsthand. He had some disturbing news for the boy's parents. "Your son is a feral or wild child. This is a phenomenon that we rarely see, but there are other instances of children who were also raised in the wild by animals. I have seen documented cases of people who were raised by dogs, badgers and wolves," said Dr. VanDyke.

"So what can we do for him?" Anna asked.

"Since the boy was taken at such a young age, it would be virtually impossible to rehabilitate him fully. He has not learned much, if any, language and probably has few memories of you speaking to him the first nine months of his life. His thought patterns are those of a wolf, and I do not feel that living in your home is in his best interest or yours. You also must think of your other children. There are homes that can care for him and help him to achieve a certain level of normalcy."

8

"No, I won't hear of it. He is staying with us! Please tell us, Dr. VanDyke, how can we help our son? What can we do for him here with his family?" cried Anna.

"I know of a child psychologist who might be able to help you make some modifications to Steven's behavior. I will also give you some medications that you can mix with his food to help with his violent outbursts. That is the best I can offer you right now," replied the doctor.

More medication? More doctors? Anna and Kevin were so frustrated. They had Steven home with the family, but he wasn't their son at all. At least he didn't realize he was their son. They continued to pray for another miracle, and they were determined not to lock their son away in an institution.

Dr. Swanson, a child psychologist, visited the family next. She recommended a system of rewards and punishments to give Steven in order to better control his behavior. "I don't want to sound cruel, but I want you to approach this as if you were training a dog. You will use food as his primary reward, and a swift striking on his nose for inappropriate actions. Since Steven is motivated by hunger, giving or withholding food from him would be the most effective intervention for the time being. I would only strike him if he is causing harm to himself or someone else," she suggested.

The Grahams thanked her for coming and stood at the doorway as she drove off. They held each other for the longest time. "Train him like a dog?" Kevin asked.

"I know. I don't like it either, but what else can we do?" his wife cried.

The grief-stricken parents consulted other specialists, but they heard the same discouraging prognosis over and over again. Steven's behavior improved slightly, but things were still very difficult for the family. The sedatives, in combination with the system of rewards and punishments, helped a little, but there was still a lot of tension in the home. Steven would soil the carpets and "mark his territory." He continued to avoid humans, but he would approach them slowly if they held out food to him.

Their efforts seemed to be working slightly, and they thought they could keep Steven in the home and see gradual improvements in his behavior over time. Then a nearly catastrophic event changed everything.

In the middle of the night, Kevin and Anna woke up to a blood-curdling scream. They ran into baby Jack's room where they saw Steven leaning over his brother's crib and biting the helpless child on his leg. Kevin grabbed the crazed boy and wrestled him back into his room. He shut the door and went to get the syringe that was to be used in emergencies. Meanwhile, Anna tended to the frantic baby and cleaned up his wound.

When things were finally settled again, Anna and Kevin lay in bed, but neither one could sleep. "This cannot go on, sweetheart," said Kevin.

"I won't hear of it. Don't say it," said Anna.

"Honey, I know you don't want to put him in an institution, but if we could find a nice place for him close by, we could visit often. Maybe they can give him the help that he needs. He is putting our other children in danger. How would you feel if he seriously injured or even killed little Jack or Kate? You would never forgive yourself, and neither would I. It is something we have to consider," Kevin said as tears streamed down his face.

"OK, I will think about it," said Anna. And they both lay in bed, unable to sleep, wondering what would become of their little boy.

The Grahams decided they would have to lock Steven in his room at night so that they could get some sleep and protect the other children. One night they awoke at 3:00 a.m. to strange noises coming from Steven's room. It was as if the boy was crying. They unlocked the door to find him pacing back and forth in front of his window. Anna looked outside and, to her horror, saw two wolves standing in their back yard and staring directly at her. "Go away! Leave us alone. Get!" she yelled. "They are coming for him, you know. They want him back," Kevin said.

"Well, they cannot have him!" Anna proclaimed defiantly.

Over the next two weeks, Anna and Kevin didn't speak to each other much. The tension in the home was tangible. Sleepless nights and exhausting days were taking their toll on the young family. They both knew that putting Steven in a group home was probably the best thing for everyone, but making that final decision was one of the hardest things they ever had to do. They eventually found a place that would take him, and it was only an hour away. The couple told themselves it was a temporary solution, and that some day, Steven could come back home. After much thought and prayer, they decided to take Steven there on that Friday morning. Ironically, he would be leaving home on his sixth birthday.

Thursday had been an incredibly difficult day for everyone, especially Anna. She was beside herself the entire day and wondering how she was going to go through with the decision to give up her son.

Anna stood by the window as she watched the neighborhood children playing outside. This is where Steven belonged, running and playing with friends and enjoying his childhood. Instead he was locked in a world where no one could reach him. Feelings of sorrow and bitterness began to rise up within her. She could not give in to these feelings, which threatened to swallow her into a large black hole. Her son had been robbed of his childhood, and she and her husband had been robbed of their son. Anna absolutely did not know what to do.

When it was time for Steven to go to bed, she spent time alone with him in his room. During the night, she would often go see her boy, rub his back, and stroke his brown curls. It was the only time she could have close contact with him. This night was especially difficult for her, and she didn't want to leave his side.

"Oh Steven, I love you so. I wish that I could let you know that. I long for you to run into my arms and let me hug you and kiss you. I have missed you for so long, and it is good to have you home, but it is not working. I cannot reach you. You are in your own little world. Please know that I love you. I hope some day you will be able to understand just how much." With those words she kissed his cheek as her tears fell onto his face. Then she curled up on the floor and cried out to God.

"Lord, I thank you for giving me my son back. You have answered our prayers. Now I have to send him away, and I don't know if I can do that. Give me the wisdom and strength to do what I need to do. Please, please help me to reach him. If there is something else that I can do that I haven't done, then let me know. I want him to know that he is our little boy, and that we love him. Give me the strength to face what I have to. But Lord, I cannot bear to lose him all over again. Amen." As she lay curled up on Steven's floor, she cried herself to sleep.

Friday came, and it was time to take Steven to his new home. The babysitter arrived to watch Kate and Jack. Kevin and Anna gave Steven a sedative that would relax him without putting him to sleep completely. It was time to go.

As they were driving along, they passed their church. Anna yelled, "Stop! Turn around and go back. I want to see Reverend White."

"Why? You can talk to him after we take Steven to the group home. I think it would help to talk to our pastor then. It would comfort you," responded Kevin.

"No, we must see him now. Please turn around," Anna pleaded.

They took Steven into the church and asked to see Reverend White. The silver-haired pastor was more than happy to visit with the family. He had been one of many staunch supporters who had helped the family through their recent difficulties. "What can I do for you?" said the pastor in his soothing voice. "Reverend White, we were on our way to take Steven to the group home, and I just felt very strongly to come in to the church. I just don't know if I can do this. I don't want to lose my son all over again. Can you help us?" cried Anna.

Reverend White held Anna's hand and felt the pain of this young mother. He had prayed for the family on numerous occasions, but this was the first time he had really seen the boy up close. Steven sat between his parents and chewed on a bone. It was one thing that could pacify the boy for hours without sedating him.

The pastor looked at the child with such compassion. He knew that his parents loved him just as he was, but they also knew all that he could be. The boy was locked in a world that no one could seem to penetrate. Reverend White silently prayed for wisdom, and then he had an idea.

He walked into his office briefly and came back. In his hand was a small mirror that he showed to Steven. The boy seemed fascinated with the object as it was shiny and small enough to handle. The pastor took the mirror and showed Steven his face. He wanted to make sure that Steven understood that he was the one reflected in the glass. At first he looked behind the mirror as if to see the person hiding behind it. He then touched it and watched inquisitively as his finger pressed up against the glass. He continued to touch the mirror and then bring his fingers to his face. Finally Steven seemed to understand that the reflection was his. He then began to make a variety of different faces in the mirror as he studied each one intently.

Reverend White then put the mirror in front of Steven's father, then back to Steven. This exchange went on for several minutes. Kevin began to imitate the faces that Steven had made. The boy's agitation was waning as his curiosity grew. He was beyond the point of fascination with the mirror. Something else was beginning to happen.

Steven began to stare intently at his reflection. The boy stopped looking in the mirror and looked at his father. He reached up and touched his dad's face, then touched his own face in the same manner. He touched his father's hair, then ran his fingers through his own. He touched Kevin's cheek, which was now wet with tears. Then the epiphany came that everyone had hoped and prayed for. Steven did not have the words to speak aloud, but his parents could read his face. It said *I'm not a wolf. I'm a boy, and I look like my father.*

"Happy birthday, son," Kevin whispered. Anna hugged Steven as tears of joy flowed down her face. For the first time since he came home, the little boy let his mother hold him. The wall that kept Steven in deception for years had crumbled before their eyes. It was time to take him home.

The journey to healing had begun. Kevin and Anna had renewed energy and hope as they raised Steven to know his true identity. They poured life into him daily. He began to understand his place in the family, and he was like a little sponge absorbing everything around him in a fresh new way. Over time, his wolf-like behaviors diminished until they were gone altogether. Steven became a big brother to his younger siblings. He learned language, and eventually went to school. He grew up to be an amazing young man who defied the odds against him, and he very much resembled his father ... and his mother. Everything that had been taken from Kevin and Anna had been restored, and they rejoiced daily in God's miraculous answer to their prayers. Their little boy had finally come home.

Chapter 2

IDENTITY THEFT

I dentity theft is currently a huge problem in our society. Through cyberspace, someone can steal another's identity and wreak havoc on his credit, bank accounts and personal life. Many Christians, however, are experiencing an identity crisis of their own. A critical identity issue they face lies in not knowing who they are and whose they are. This is the biggest challenge that people in the Body of Christ face today.

Identity lets people know who they are. It gives them purpose and meaning in life. Identity defines individuals and their relationship to their surroundings. Having an incorrect view of himself nearly ruined Steven's life, and it brought heartache to those around him. When he realized that he was a little boy, a total change for his life was set in motion. It put him on a new path. Understanding his identity as a human, not a wolf, was critical in helping Steven know who he was and to whom he belonged.

If knowing one's identity is so important, then what defines a Christian's identity? John writes, "How great is the love the Father has lavished on us, that we should be called children of God! And that is what we are!" (1 John 3:1). As His children, believers share in the character of their heavenly Father. They are like Him. Christians also have an inheritance from the One who created the world. Identity lets them know they belong to Him and that they are loved.

Children should not have to earn love from their parents. In our fallen world, however, many parents aren't able to love in this way. But God is the perfect parent who loves His children unconditionally simply because they belong to Him. As His children, they also need to recognize that they have been placed in a family of other believers. Christians can enjoy fellowship with their brothers and sisters in Christ as part of the family of God.

Because they are part of God's family, they have the assurance of spending eternity with their Father. That sense of security is like a well-worn blanket that envelops them and empowers them to face each day with the presence of their loving Father within them.

Finally, identity gives Christians position as they are "in Christ," and He dwells in them. There is freedom in knowing that believers don't have to perform for Him; instead He performed for His children. (For more on who believers are in Christ, please see "Identity Verses" at the end of this book.)

Recognizing that he was not a wolf freed Steven to live out who he really was—a human being. What makes a person human? DNA has everything to do with it. Where does a child get his DNA? His parents. Steven is person because his parents are people. When they were looking forward to his birth, they didn't pray for a human. They did not wonder if he was going to be a puppy or a kitten. No, they were expecting a boy or girl human. Pigs give birth to pigs; dogs give birth to dogs, and so on. This is the way God designed nature. And, unless humans intervene and tamper with His plan of creation, that is the way it will always be.

Humans' actions have no impact on their identity. If they opt to walk on all fours and drink water from the dog dish, that does not make them dogs. If they lick their paws, purr and eat cat food, it doesn't make them cats. People may stare at them and wonder what in the world they are doing, but their actions don't change who they really are.

In the story, Steven acted like a wolf. He howled; he did not walk upright, but those actions did not change who he truly was inside. Birth determined his identity, and his parents were humans, not wolves. However, Steven did not know that. He had been misled into thinking that he was a wolf, not a little boy. Through that deception, he started acting like the person (or in this case animal) that he believed himself to be. His ignorance of truth kept him from becoming everything God designed him to be.

This reality applies to the Christian life as well. People are born into the physical world, and they receive their spiritual DNA from their father, Adam. Through him, sin entered the rest of humanity as a result of the Fall. When individuals are born-again, however, they then receive the spiritual DNA of their heavenly Father and His Son Jesus. Since Jesus was conceived by the Holy Spirit—and not of man—sin never entered into Him.

Jesus led a perfect life, never sinned, and operated in complete and total love and obedience to His Father, God. In Romans 5:12–21, Paul talks about sin entering through Adam and exiting through Jesus. Through Christ, Christians receive righteousness which only comes through faith in Him (Romans 3:22). Their spiritual heritage was changed when they accepted the gift of salvation through Christ. Physical DNA cannot change, but spiritual DNA can! Their father was once Adam, but now believers have a new dad, and His name is Jesus.

Paul continued this line of thought when he wrote, "The first man was of the dust of the earth, the second man from heaven. As was the earthly man, so are those who are of the earth; and as is the man from heaven, so also are those who are of heaven. And just as we have borne the likeness of the earthly man, so shall we bear the likeness of the man from heaven" (1 Corinthians 15:47–49). In other words, Paul is saying, "You look like your Father, and you have received His righteousness, now live it out." When believers receive (acknowledge) their identity as children of God, then they place a new label on themselves.

Labels affect how people perceive their identity. These labels can come from a variety of sources, from home to work to school. I taught in the public school system for seventeen years. While in the classroom, I saw the positive and negative aspects of labeling children. If a teacher gave a positive label to a child, such as "gifted," then the child would most likely live up to that expectation. On the other hand, if the teacher gave a student a negative label, such as "behavioral disorder" or "learning disability," then the child would often live "down" to that label.

There have been many studies in which teachers were told that a certain group was "gifted" while another group was "slow." Children were placed in groups randomly without taking their abilities into consideration; however, the teachers were not aware of this fact.

The studies showed time after time that the label created a self-fulfilling prophecy. If the teacher believed a child was gifted, he had a set of expectations that were higher for that child than he had for the other children. The teacher made sure the student succeeded by speaking life to him. ("Johnny, you are a very smart boy, and I know you can figure this out. Let's try again.")

If the teacher believed the child had behavioral or educational deficiencies, those lower expectations most usually caused the child to fit the perception of the teacher. ("Susie, I know you are slow in math. Let me give you some easier problems." "Billy, you are such a troublemaker; why are you so bad?") The children lived out or manifested the behavior of the labels, whether positive or negative, that had been attached to them.

The biblical explanation for this phenomenon is found in Proverbs: "For as he thinks in his heart, so is he" (Proverbs 23:7 NKJV). Label someone a loser, and he will lose. Label someone a winner, and he will win. That is, if the person receives (takes to himself) the label given to him or her. If someone calls me a loser, I can do nothing about that. But if I receive that label for myself—or put it on—then I will act accordingly. I will lose.

Many caregivers, educators, coaches, parents and other adults may try to motivate a young person by calling him a "loser" in order to get him to do better. They think that by calling someone a loser, he won't like that label and will therefore try harder. This will make him want to be a winner, they rationalize.

However, that is not true. Actually, the exact opposite will usually happen. When an adult labels a child a loser, and the child receives that negative label, he will act like the person he believes himself to be. The kid will see himself as a failure, which will result in him becoming a loser in his mind. He may have episodes of "winning," but they will be short-lived because the child has internalized himself as a loser—and losers lose.

When trying to motivate children, my former co-teachers and I consistently tried to build a child's confidence and self-esteem. Teachers get very upset when a student of high ability performs poorly on daily assignments and exams. When educators see wasted potential, it gets their feathers ruffled quickly. I remember many students with great ability who did poorly and even failed school altogether. We'd give them pep talks to build their confidence and try to get them excited about doing better. And, voilà, the student would ace a test or start improving in some area, and we felt that we were on the right track to getting the student on the road to success.

Almost every time, though, the success was temporary. The celebration soon turned to frustration when the student exhibited the former poor performance levels and began to fail again. We would scratch our heads and wonder why the student, after tasting success, went right back to his old ways.

God has revealed the answer in His Word. Proverbs 23:7, particularly the wording in the New King James Version—"For as he thinks in his heart, so is he"—reveals that people perform at the level at which they see themselves. Unless the students have a revelation on the inside that they are indeed a success, achieving external results will only seem like a fluke. They will return to their comfort zone and think: *I did well that time, but I'm still a loser. This won't last.*

On the bright side, children who see themselves as winners may experience bouts of failure. However, this does not consume or define them. They will see it as a temporary situation—a setback—and their perception of themselves will influence the outcome. A child will subconsciously think: *I failed on this assignment, but I am a winner. I will do better next time. This doesn't define me.*

This idea applies to adults as well. Many people of all ages have been robbed of their identity. They have been told by someone (parent, teacher, coach, spouse, ex, and so on) that they will never amount to anything—that they are worthless. If somebody receives that label, then negative actions will follow as a result.

Society can also have an adverse impact on how people see themselves. When people—even Christians—buy into the media's philosophy that says beauty looks like this, and success looks like that, they are prone to see themselves negatively.

How many people struggle with their self-worth as they are bombarded daily with messages that the world gives them?

In order to have a healthy self-image, believers need to see themselves as God sees them. When Christians let God define them, they will discover their true identity in Christ and become all that He created them to be.

How does God define His children? The apostle Peter writes, "But you are a chosen people, a royal priesthood, a holy nation, a people belonging to God, that you may declare the praises of him who called you out of darkness into his wonderful light. Once you were not a people, but now you are the people of God; once you had not received mercy, but now you have received mercy" (1 Peter 2:9–10).

God's people should be walking advertisements that demonstrate how He takes care of His children! Walking in the light includes receiving the new identity God has richly bestowed on His followers. Christians need to see themselves as "a royal priesthood" whom He has set apart for His glory (Ephesians 1:11–12)!

Studying genealogy has become an interesting hobby—even an obsession for some. I love history and would find it very interesting to learn about my ancestors. What if I were to go into the archives and discover that I came from a bunch of bank robbers? I might think to myself: *I have the sudden and strange compulsion to rob a bank!* I might view myself negatively because of my questionable heritage. The power of suggestion could influence me greatly unless I held firmly to who I really am—regardless of my ancestral heritage.

On the other hand, what if I discovered that I came from royalty? My countenance would change. I would begin to lift my head and straighten my back just a bit—maybe even hold up my pinkie when I drink tea. I might think: *I feel like putting on a crown. Now I know why!*

A few years ago, a story surfaced of a young girl who discovered she was an African princess. The young woman had struggled with identity issues for years, yet when she was in her late 20s, she got a call from her biological father telling her she was descended from royalty. What an amazing story!

Yet this is what has happened to each and every believer in Christ. Sinners can go back through their spiritual genealogy and find Adam, the man into whom original sin first entered. This is very discouraging news, but wait! When people are born anew, they become saints, and their spiritual heritage will take them back to Jesus, the one who took away the sins of the whole world (1 John 2:2). That should cause Christians to lift their chin and walk with dignity and determination to live out the wonderful heritage they have received through Christ. Believers got the call from their heavenly Father, and He told them they are princes and princesses—children of the King!

I recently watched a documentary on slavery that demonstrates this concept of identity and its powerful impact on a person's life. The narrator took famous African-Americans and researched their ancestry back to slave times in the United States. Time and time again I watched the countenance of these well-known people change as they discovered their rich heritage. The pride they felt was evident in their faces as they discovered these life-changing revelations.

One man in particular—a young actor—learned that his great-great-grandfather had once served as one of our nation's first African-American congressman. The young man said he never knew he had such an ambitious and successful man in his family. He also commented that had he known this information at a younger age, it would have changed his life for the better. He believed it would have inspired him to make something of his life at a time when he thought he would amount to nothing. This knowledge gave him a sense of dignity that had eluded him for years.

Understanding heritage can truly change people's lives and influence them to follow in the footsteps of those who have gone before them. Christians need to take a closer look at their spiritual heritage as well. As believers, that journey will take them back to Jesus, the Author and Finisher ("Perfecter") of their faith (Hebrews 12:2). What about you? Who or what has defined you as a person? Are you known for being someone's spouse, sibling, child, or parent? What happens when the spouse leaves, the siblings move away, the parents pass on, and the children move out of the nest? Many people suffer when the foundation of their identity cracks. The entire house can topple when these life-changing events occur. Perhaps a mid-life crisis is really an identity crisis in disguise.

As a believer, if you have built your house upon the Rock, you have a solid foundation that will never be shaken (Psalm 18:2). If you see yourself as His child, that is one thing that will never change about you. Your identity has been placed on the sure foundation of Jesus Christ. There is peace, assurance and life when He is the cornerstone, and those who trust in Him will never be put to shame (1 Peter 2:6).

Steven learned that his father was Kevin Graham. That revelation changed his life and put him on a path to true self-discovery. My father is Jesus Christ, the King of kings and Lord of lords. That makes me a princess. You, too, can receive the same spiritual heritage by simply accepting Christ as your personal Savior. Don't let the enemy or anyone else rob you of your identity.

Let God define you by becoming His child; then you will live out who you really are. If you have already received Christ as your personal Savior, then it is time to discover your true identity and the glorious riches and divine power that God has placed on the inside of you (2 Peter 1:3). You will be amazed at what you find.

Chapter 3

SPLIT PERSONALITY?

Many Christians seem to be suffering from a split personality disorder. Because they don't know who they really are, they can become confused by conflicting behaviors and feelings. The Christian walk can seem like a roller coaster ride with enough ups and downs to make believers sick to their stomachs.

In many different songs, people sing lyrics like, "I'm a saint, and I'm a sinner." They picture themselves with an "angelic" miniature version on one shoulder and the "devilish" one on the other. The problem with that line of thinking is that a person is either a saint or a sinner. The way a person acts does not often line up with his identity. However, knowing one's true identity will greatly affect how a person acts.

Steven certainly had some conflicting feelings as he wrestled with who he was. (He might have sung, "I'm a wolf, and I'm a boy"—which cannot be true.) Perhaps when he lived in the wolf den, he thought, *I don't really look like they do. They are all furry, and I have very little hair. Do I really belong here? Who am I?*

Did he notice that he couldn't run nearly as fast as they did, or that his teeth weren't very sharp? Did he have inklings of his humanity? It is difficult to read the thoughts of someone in that condition, but one has to wonder if any of these questions crossed his mind when he believed himself to be a wolf.

After Steven realized his true identity, he started acting like a human being. In the early stages of his new life, he probably had several setbacks. Maybe after walking upright on a regular basis, he suddenly started crawling around on the floor and eating out of the dog dish. Did that make him a wolf? No, his identity never changed even when he acted like an animal. He was always 100% human; he just didn't always walk out who he really was. The challenge is not to make him "more human" but to get him to be the person he was created to be. Until he became established in his new identity, he probably suffered a lot of confusion and defeat.

Why do so many Christians struggle with conflicting feelings of their own? The answer can be found in the Bible. The apostle Paul says, "May God himself, the God of peace, sanctify you through and through. May your whole spirit, soul and body be kept blameless at the coming of our Lord Jesus Christ. The one who call you is faithful and he will do it" (1 Thessalonians 5:23–24). These verses reveal that believers are made of three parts: spirit, soul, and body.

Before a person receives Christ as Savior, his spirit is dead to God. It happened as a result of the Fall. God warned Adam and Eve that if they ate of the tree of the knowledge of good and evil, they would surely die (Genesis 2:17). Did they die physically when they ate the fruit? No, they died spiritually. The word "death" really means separation. When a person dies, he is separated from life. In this case, death meant a separation from God.

Several years ago, a student where I was teaching wore a shirt that said, "I see dead people." It was taken from a popular movie at the time and was meant to be shocking. To me, it was no big deal. That is because I see dead people all the time—spiritually dead people, that is. Anyone who has not accepted Jesus Christ as Savior has a dead spirit and is therefore dead to God. This is a sad but true reality in the world today. A person with a dead spirit cannot understand the things of God or relate to Him. Many people in this condition might plan to figure God out first and then decide whether or not to receive Him. However, no one can ever figure God out because the world says that seeing is believing, and God says that believing is seeing.

When a person accepts the gift of eternal life through Jesus Christ by faith, his spirit comes alive. His spiritual eyes are opened to the amazing things of God the moment he is born anew. Those who were once spiritually blind now see.

God is spirit, and believers must worship him in spirit and in truth (John 4:24). God relates to believers in their born-again spirits. Because He is spirit, that is the only way that He can relate to a Christian—spirit to spirit. This new spirit is absolutely perfect and sealed. That means that nothing gets in, and nothing gets out. Sin cannot even penetrate it!

Imagine a jar of peaches—the kind that Grandma used to can every summer. If a person dips the sealed jar in mud, the mud cannot come through the seal. If someone immerses the jar in water, the peaches won't escape. They are sealed in and protected. It is the same with the born-again spirit (Ephesians 1:13). The bad stuff cannot get in, and the good stuff cannot escape.

Verse 14 goes on to say that this Holy Spirit is a deposit that guarantees the believer's inheritance. The born-again spirit of a Christian became one with the Lord at his conversion (1 Corinthians 6:17). This completed work was accomplished by Jesus

Christ on the cross. His followers must accept this gift by faith, not by their own works or efforts (Romans 3:22).

The born-again spirit is described in many verses in the Bible. Paul writes, "Therefore, if anyone is in Christ, he is a new creation; the old has gone, the new has come!" (2 Corinthians 5:17). The symbol for this verse is a butterfly, which represents a totally new creation completely different from the way it was before. An amazing metamorphosis has occurred.

Can a butterfly ever go back to being a caterpillar? No, it cannot happen. Yet some believers seem to think they can go back and forth between being a butterfly and a caterpillar. Life doesn't work that way. The same kind of total transformation happens to a sinner when he receives Christ and becomes a saint. Where does that instantaneous change occur? In the born-again spirit.

God is holy and can only indwell a perfectly clean and spotless vessel. In the Old Testament, that place was the Ark of the Covenant. It was placed in the Temple in an area known as the Holy of Holies. Only the priest could enter into this sanctuary, which he did once a year, to offer sacrifices for the sins of the people.

Jesus came to obtain eternal redemption once and for all through His shed blood (Hebrews 9:12). Under the New Covenant, the Holy Spirit lives on the inside of every believer. The Christian's spirit represents the most holy place where God now resides. That is why it must be absolutely perfect and free from sin. Nothing can enter this place but God Himself. Again, believers' spirits are perfect and sealed. When Christians realize they are the temple of the living God, then that should make a huge impact on their identities!

The next part of a human is the soul. This includes a person's mind, will and emotions. Another word for soul is personality. The spirit of a believer never changes, but the soul is in the process of continual change, sometimes for the better and other times for the worse. The will determines what a person does and believes. It is extremely powerful. It can decide to accept Christ or reject Him. God desires to be part of individuals' lives, but because He gives them a free will, He will not force Himself on people. However, the Lord does not want anyone to perish but to find everlasting life (2 Peter 3:9).

The mind is where the battle really takes place. Christians wage war in their minds, not in their spirits. The spirit never changes and is always in agreement with God and His Word. The spirit is constantly rejoicing in Him.

On the other hand, the mind will go wherever a person chooses to let it go. "Set your minds on things above, not on earthly things. For you died, and your life is now hidden with Christ in God" (Colossians 3:2–3). The word "set" is a command that indicates there is a choice to be made. Individuals have to decide what they will think about, and Paul lists out several topics in Philippians 4:8–9 for them to meditate on: things that are noble, right, pure, lovely, admirable, and so on.

People will respond to whatever they set their minds on. When people focus on godly things, they will have stability despite their circumstances. The mind controlled by the Spirit is life and peace (Romans 8:6). But what kinds of things do individuals usually allow themselves to think about? Their performance? Sin? Worries and anxieties? The negative events of this world? No wonder many Christians are so discouraged and confused!

The key to winning the battle of the mind is given to Christians by Paul: "Do not conform any longer to the pattern of this world, but be transformed by the renewing of your mind. Then you will be able to test and approve what God's will is—his good, pleasing and perfect will" (Romans 12:2). In order to fully discover who they really are, believers must renew their minds in the Word of God on a regular basis. (For more on this subject, please see "Identity Verses" at the end of this book.)

It is not always easy, but the results are well worth it. That is where Steven will find victory. He was given his humanness at his birth. That was a gift, so to speak, from his parents. In other words, he didn't earn it. However, he had to keep telling himself who he was: *I'm not a wolf; I'm a boy, and this is what boys do*. Like Steven, Christians receive their identity as a gift of God's grace by faith, not through works so that no one can boast (Ephesians 2:8–9).

God also created people to have emotions as part of their soul. If individuals were to go through life as unfeeling robots, it would not be very rewarding. Emotions like elation and contentment make life more enjoyable. On the other hand, feelings such as depression or grief can make life unbearable at times. People's emotions can go up and down like a roller coaster. Emotions react to what a person sets his mind on.

Let me illustrate. Have you ever watched a scary movie? You might be in the comfort of your own home with the door locked and a baseball bat under your couch. When you focus on something scary, what happens? Your body reacts as if it is in danger. Your heart begins to pound; your palms sweat; and your knees go weak. Adrenaline is released in your body, and you are ready to fight or flee. Are you in danger? No, but your emotions do not know this. Your body begins to react as if you were in danger. Why does this happen? Because you set your mind on a scary thing even though it was not real.

The same thing happens to believers. When they set their minds on the wrong things, their emotions react negatively. People often set their minds on circumstances instead of God. Then they send up prayers for God to change their circumstances, but He wants to change them within the circumstances. By focusing on God, believers are able to put problems in the proper perspective. He has given Christians His power to overcome the situations that they face in life (1 John 5:4–5). This divine power has given believers everything they need for life and godliness (2 Peter 1:3). When people are anchored to Him, they cannot get blown all over the place by what happens in this ever-changing and tumultuous world.

God gave humans emotions, and there is nothing wrong with them. Jesus experienced the same emotions we have such as anger, joy, fear, and sorrow. They can be wonderful, but they should not have free rein in our lives. They should be the caboose and not the engine. In other words, feelings should be the last to line up, not the thing that drives the train. All too often, people put their emotions in control of their lives, and the result becomes: "If it feels good, do it." However, feelings do not know right from wrong—they cannot think. Emotions should never be put in charge! Did Steven feel like a wolf? Of course, he did. Did that make him a wolf? Absolutely not. Feelings do not determine who believers are, and they should not control what they do!

In the world today, many people encourage others to walk by feelings. They might tell Steven, "Hey, if you feel like a wolf, then just go with it. Who am I to tell you if you're a wolf or not? The choice is yours. Live and let live, you know."

This kind of mind-set would rob Steven of all that he could be and all that he could accomplish by receiving his true identity as a human being. These thoughts would keep him in bondage because they are lies. Many people's lives are in a complete mess because they followed their feelings and did what they felt was right. Faith and feelings are polar opposites.

This is where many lack victory in their Christian walk. They use feelings as a barometer to determine what is happening and then make decisions based on them. Walking by faith is the only way to overcome this. Faith is the evidence of things hoped for and certainty of what cannot be seen (Hebrews 11:1). I may not always feel loved, but the Word of God says that I am. I may not always feel happy, but God's Word says that I have joy. I may not always feel forgiven, but the Word of God says that my sins were paid for by Jesus. What determines identity? Birth (either physical or spiritual)—not actions, performance, or feelings!

Once Steven realized who he was, there were probably times that he still felt like a wolf. Some event, like a full moon, might trigger that emotion. However, if he continually renewed his mind with the truth of his real identity, those feelings would eventually line up with reality. Again, feelings should be the last thing to get on board. Eventually they will line up, but it might take awhile. The more a person renews his mind in God's Word, the quicker it will happen.

Understanding that believers are made up of three parts is vital to a victorious Christian walk. This knowledge helps people to understand themselves better and the Word of God more clearly. For example, John writes, "In this way, love is made complete among us so that we will have confidence on the day of judgment, because in this world we are like him," (1 John 4:17). Believers are like Jesus in this world? If they do not understand spirit, soul and body, this verse could condemn them. Many mistakenly believe that they have "missed the mark" and try to start acting more like Jesus. For those who have received Christ, they could never miss the mark. Jesus is the bull's eye!

Followers of Christ cannot "think" their way into acting more like Jesus on their own. Instead, they are to live out who they already are in their born-again spirit as believers. Instead of saying WWJD (What would Jesus do?), Christians should say WDJD (What did Jesus do?). He placed His Spirit within every one of His followers, which is their new identity in Christ. This is the new position from which they are to operate and relate to God. It is a position of absolute victory! A verse like 1 John 4:17 should bring victory because it refers to a believer's born-again spirit, which is perfect. Once that revelation is received, then holy actions will follow.

When someone understands that he has already achieved perfection in his born-again spirit, and the soul lines up with that truth by the renewing of the mind, what comes next? His body will get on board as well.

Imagine the peace and freedom that would come from knowing that the spirit is already perfect! That is a Christian's real identity and how God relates to him. His emotions will become more calm and stable because of the peace that he has in his spirit. When his emotions are in control because of the calmness in his spirit, then his body will relax, which results in a healthier person on many levels.

A misunderstanding of a believer's true identity in Christ hurts him or her not only emotionally but also physically. It affects the body in many destructive ways. For example, I recently heard that the number one medicine prescribed in the United States is an anti-depressant.

Why are so many people in such a blessed and prosperous nation depressed? I believe it is because people don't know who they are. They are so wrapped up in their feelings they cannot see truth. Stress caused by this misunderstanding has also caused a multitude of health problems from digestive issues, to heart problems, to headaches. Why are people so stressed out? They are trying to figure out who they are, and they are trying to earn their self-worth instead of just receiving it. People have negative feelings as a direct result of thinking negative thoughts. This adversely affects their bodies.

The world is completely consumed with making the body look good. From fitness programs, to plastic surgery, to diet plans, people are going to great lengths to make themselves look better on the outside. However, the body is a reflection of what a person is feeling on the inside. Improving one's external appearance will not evoke true change in the heart. For example, many people struggle with weight, but people who lose a significant number of pounds still look in the mirror and see an overweight person. Why? Proverbs 23:7, the way the New King James Version states it, again has the answer: "As a person thinks in his heart, so is he." Once Christians understand who they are in the spirit, then renew their minds in accordance with that truth, the body will line up. It is the last thing to get on board not the first!

I recently heard a dynamic speaker make a powerful statement. He said, "The problem with Christians is that they keep praying to get into a room they're already in." That statement resonated within me. What is the "room"? I believe it has many names including forgiveness, acceptance, value, redemption, love, and salvation. God's Word says that His children already have those gifts and much, much more through His Son, Jesus Christ. Once that revelation travels the furthest distance in the world—from the brain to the heart—then that life will flow from believers out to a lost world that needs to hear and receive these truths as well. What a shame it is that so many Christians are trying to get what they already have!

What if Steven looked at himself in the mirror and began condemning himself for not being "human enough"? He might look outside at kids his age playing games and going to school. He might think, *If I were only more human, I could be like them.* Again, he doesn't need to change his identity, but he needs a revelation of what he already has! The same holds true for many believers today.

"His divine power has given us everything we need for life and godliness through our knowledge of him who called us by his own glory and goodness" (2 Peter 1:3). In this verse, everything means, well, everything. Believers lack nothing except the realization of what they have in Christ. How do Christians receive this "everything"? Through the knowledge of Him. Did Steven lack anything as a human? No, but he did lack the knowledge of who he was. Multitudes of Christ's followers face the same challenge today.

Many followers of Christ think they need to become more spiritual. What they truly need is a revelation that their born again spirit is already perfect and will not change. This represents their true identity, and it is in Christ. That truth then needs to filter through to the soul and body. One of the most misunderstood verses in the bible is Philippians 2:12 where Paul tells believers to work out their salvation with fear and trembling. In many other verses, Paul made it very clear that salvation comes by faith in Christ alone and not by works. Did Paul contradict himself?

What does it mean to work out your salvation? I believe Paul is telling followers of Christ to let the truth of their perfect spirit work its way out and infiltrate and then transform the rest of their beings. In other words, they must be diligent about letting that life of God flow into their soul (mind, will, emotions) and their bodies. This is how to achieve true transformation and victory as believers. For Steven, he will become all that he can be only by letting his true identity transform his personality and his body as well. He doesn't need to be more human, only to act out who he already is. It is no different for Christians today.

What about you? Do you have a life of peace? Have you judged your relationship with God based on your performance or His? When you were all upset because you thought that you had failed God, He was looking at you in your perfect spirit which looked exactly like Jesus! You thought you were a worm, but God saw a butterfly. Stop trying to earn what you already have. Just receive who God made you to be, and everything else will then line up from there. Stop crawling around in the mud with worms and use your wings to fly!

Proverbs 14:30 says, "A heart at peace gives life to the body." Being in a relationship with God and knowing that Christians are right with Him through the finished work of Jesus can give them the peace they are searching for in life. Believers are made up of a spirit, soul and body. Their spirits are alive to God, 100% perfect, and sealed. When individuals' souls and bodies line up with that truth, there will be no more thoughts of a split personality. They are complete in Christ and absolutely healthy and whole.

Chapter 4

The Horse and the Cart

Many people have heard the saying, "Don't put the cart before the horse." In the old days, a horse would pull a cart behind it. This made life much easier in the era before modern technology. If the cart came first, the horse would have to push it, which was obviously not very efficient.

How does this apply to the life of a Christian? Identity is the horse. It is designed to pull the cart, which in this case is a person's behavior. When believers know who they are in Christ, their actions will naturally follow as a result. But if they let their actions influence their identity, they are putting the cart first.

As soon as Steven realized who he really was, then appropriate actions followed. Attempts to mold his behavior first then get it to influence his identity simply did not work. The bottom line is this: An individual will act like the person he believes himself to be.

As a whole, Christians need to stop trying to change their behavior and that of others without a revelation of true identity! How many times have believers preached to sinners about their outward behavior? How effective have those efforts been? True change works its way from the inside out.

I recently heard someone say, "You cannot change your condition without first understanding your position." That is a very accurate statement. Once a person understands his position in Christ, then his condition (how he lives) will naturally change as a result of knowing who and where he is.

What is the believer's position? He has been adopted into God's family. Ephesians 1:4–5 describes how believers were called to be holy and blameless in His sight and that they were adopted as sons of God through Jesus Christ. Christians need to have a revelation of their position as children of God.

In the story, Steven must recognize his position within his family in order to fully understand who he really is. Because he is Kevin and Anna's child, he has certain rights, privileges, and eventually responsibilities that come with that position. His parents will love him unconditionally, not for what he can do for them, but because he belongs to them. This lesson applies to believers' lives as well as they relate to their Father as His children.

Many Christians try to earn their position instead of simply receiving it. That is how the world works, but not how the Kingdom of God operates. What does a prince do to earn his title? He is simply born into the king's family. It is no different for Christians, the children of the King of kings.

When people know who they really are, their actions will naturally follow. I am a person, so I act like people do. Whether someone is a newborn, 10 years old, 50, or 100, that person is 100% human. When a proper identity is received, a person's actions will line up with that truth as a result.

Look at newborns. How human are they? The answer is 100%. How many human behaviors do they exhibit? Not many. They cannot walk, talk, or really care for themselves in any way. They are dependent on others to meet their every need. However, they will begin to exhibit human behaviors when raised in the proper environment. The potential is there, but it takes years to manifest.

Imagine that I am talking to a newborn. I might say, "Some day you will grow up and learn to walk and talk. You will go to school, learn to read, and have friends. As you grow up, you will be part of a family who will do fun things with you like going to the park and taking vacations. When you are old enough, you may have a job some day. Then you will have a family and perhaps children of your own. You might even decide to have a pet, like a dog, cat, fish, hamster ...."

How ridiculous would it be for me to try to tell the baby all that he will see, do and experience in life? That infant will not understand one word of it! However, most humans will eventually accomplish many of those milestones in their lives and much more.

A newborn is equipped with everything he needs for life as a human in the world. God knits humans together and blesses each one of them with an amazing body and incredible brain (Psalm 139:13). However, it takes years to develop and hone those skills and put those gifts to good use. Growing up is a beautiful process, and life should unfold into something magnificent. It just takes time.

It is the same way with a person's spiritual birth. What if I were to have a similar conversation with someone who had just been born again? I might say, "Some day you will be formed in the image of Christ. You will act holy just as Jesus is holy. Your desires will change to godly desires. You will become less selfish and care about others more than you do yourself. The love you have for God will continue to grow as you learn more about Him. Your fear of death will diminish as you begin to understand all that God has for you in heaven. You may even reach the point where you willingly lay down your life for Christ as He willingly laid down His life for you. Some day you will learn to love your enemies and even pray for those who persecute you ...."

A spiritual infant would be completely overwhelmed by this conversation! In fact, he may turn tail and run as fast as he can, wondering why he ever decided to follow Jesus in the first place. Like growing up physically, maturing in Christ is also a beautiful process that must happen over time. The tricky part lies in understanding that it is fairly easy to determine a person's chronological age and nearly impossible (and often dangerous) to try to determine a person's spiritual age.

I received Christ as an adult. Chronologically I was 30 years old, but spiritually I was just an infant. Shortly after my conversion, I heard a song on the radio with the words, "good-bye to me." Whenever that song came on, I switched stations. At the time, I was not yet ready to say good-bye to the old Michele. It seemed like a scary proposition and way out of my comfort zone. Now I would love to hear that song. I realize that to live is Christ and to die is gain (Philippians 1:21). Since I am maturing in Christ, I see the fruit of abiding in Him as I realize that my old self needed to go. In fact, I should have had a bon voyage party for her years ago. Good-bye, Michele! Don't forget to write!

Just like a newborn child, baby Christians have to find their spiritual legs and learn to walk on them. Again, the acceptance of a believer's new identity must come first, and then be followed by actions, or that tired old horse is going to struggle trying to push the cart. This process of maturation involves discovering all that Jesus did for His followers when He died on the cross and rose again more than 2,000 years ago.

Christ places His righteousness, power, love, deliverance, salvation and much more, on the inside of every believer in abundance at the moment that person accepts Him as Savior. The Christian walk is a journey where believers discover what they have received at their spiritual birth just as an infant "discovers" what he has been given at his physical birth. The process cannot be rushed, but it can be hindered. First a child sits up alone, then crawls, then walks. Something can come against the child so that this natural development does not take place, and that is what happened to Steven. Believing he was a wolf stunted his development as a human.

What can hinder a believer's maturation process? There are many factors. Those who seek God will find Him (Luke 11:9). Some believers seem content to have surface knowledge of God and do not desire to go deeper. To illustrate, I can know about George Washington, but I can never know him personally. Many people know about Jesus, but do they really know Him experientially? That is the kind of "knowing" that God wants believers to have. George Washington died hundreds of years ago, but Jesus Christ is alive and well today and can be known by His followers through His precious Holy Spirit!

Another reason that some Christians do not fully mature in Christ is because they believe that they are indebted to God. Perhaps they feel they owe Him something and cannot pay it. (If you owed someone money, would you hang around him or would you avoid him until you paid off your debt?) It is true that followers of Christ do owe God a debt they can never pay, but praise God that Jesus paid it all in full!

One large factor that keeps Christians from maturing is that many do not understand that they are totally forgiven. Jesus paid the price for the sins of the world (past, present and future) when He died on the cross. Many Christians cannot understand how God could forgive future sins. How many sins had any person living today committed when Jesus died? The answer is zero. Jesus paid the price once and for all when He died on the cross and rose again (Hebrews 9:12).

Before He gave up His life, He proclaimed, "It is finished" (John 19:30). After His resurrection, Jesus sat down at the right hand of the Father to show that His work was complete (Hebrews 1:3). This is referring to the complete and total forgiveness of sins for believers once and for all. He sat down because His work was complete. Not only that, He sat believers down with Him in heavenly realms in Jesus Christ (Ephesians 2:6). This is the position from which Christians should approach God. They are seated with Him in heavenly places!

Many Christians live in a state of continual condemnation and confession because they do not understand that all of their sins have been totally forgiven. Until believers understand the finality of what was accomplished on the cross, they will never enter into the power of the resurrection.

Through Jesus, God provided complete forgiveness which redeemed those who have received it from the curse. He brought them from the dominion of darkness into the Kingdom of the Son. God did all of this in order to bring individuals into a relationship with Him (Colossians 1:13-14). The barrier that separated God from man has been removed, and followers of Christ therefore have peace with God (Romans 5:1). Christians can now enjoy fellowship with God just like Adam and Eve did in the Garden of Eden prior to the Fall.

Paul wrote, "All this is from God, who reconciled us to himself through Christ and gave us the ministry of reconciliation: that God was reconciling the world to himself in Christ, not counting men's sins against them. And he has committed to us the message of reconciliation. We are therefore Christ's ambassadors, as though God were making his appeal through us. We implore you on Christ's behalf: Be reconciled to God. God made him who had no sin to be sin for us, so that in him we might become the righteousness of God" (2 Corinthians 5:18-21).

God provided forgiveness to restore relationship, yet some believers can be more consumed with the forgiveness of sins than on the reconciliation that they have with the Father. Imagine Steven spending a day with his dad shortly after he realized he was his son. Instead of simply enjoying his dad's company, Steven apologized for all of his shortcomings, mistakes, and failures. He could have done this more and better; he should have done that less, and so on. What if this went on for hours on end? At some point his father might say, "Okay, I forgive you already! Can we just hang out?"

The apostle Peter revealed that Christians can become ineffective and unproductive in the knowledge of the Lord because they forget that their past sins were forgiven (2 Peter 1:8–9). Who wants to be ineffective in their Christian walk? No one. But until believers realize they are completely forgiven, they will be unproductive in their witness to others. Christians must be good ambassadors for Christ!

Let's continue with this thought since it is extremely important for believers to understand. In Luke 6:37, Jesus tells His followers to forgive so they will be forgiven. Jesus was teaching this concept before the cross, so He still taught under the Law. He had not yet shed His blood for the forgiveness of sins once and for all.

When reading Scripture, it is vitally important to distinguish whether or not an event or teaching happened before or after the cross. The cross is the dividing line between the Old and New Covenants. Before the cross, sins were merely "covered over" by the sacrifices God required; after the cross, sin is forgiven.

After the death and resurrection of Christ, the apostle Paul taught that believers should forgive others as Christ forgave them (Colossians 3:13). A huge part of maturing in Christ lies in understanding the total forgiveness of sins once and for all. The word "forgave" is past tense, meaning it is something already accomplished. Praise God that He keeps no record of His children's wrongs (1 Corinthians 13:5).

Christians need to grow and mature just like children need to grow into adults over time. There are few things more beautiful than watching a newborn nursing at his mother's breast, but it is quite repulsive to watch a ten-year-old do the same. Like that child, many Christians need to be weaned!

When I go into Christian bookstores, I am amazed at how many Christian self-help books are available. Christian self-help is really an oxymoron. The Christian life should be one of God-dependence, yet the message in many books seems to be to try harder in the flesh.

God has made it very clear in His Word that human efforts by themselves will not produce the right results. John says, "The Spirit gives life; the flesh counts for nothing. The words I have spoken to you are spirit and they are life" (John 6:63).

Furthermore, the prophet Isaiah wrote, "All our righteous acts are like filthy rags; we all shrivel up like a leaf, and like the wind our sins sweep us away" (Isaiah 64:6). This man of God was referring to humans' attempts to become righteous on their own. Individuals receive the gift of righteousness only by faith (Philippians 3:9).

The self-help books encourage Christians to be "better" or "stronger"—and the readers' hearts are in the right place. However, the methods the books suggest often leave much to be desired. Many of those methods are actually counterproductive. I envision many Christians perpetually trying to get the carrot that is dangling in front of them, but it is always just out of reach. This only leads to a defeatist attitude and a boatload of condemnation. As a result, many people either try harder and fail, fake it till they make it, or give up altogether.

I can just imagine what some of the books for Steven might look like. *You Can Walk Upright Too*, *How to Become a Human God Can Use*, *Forty Days to a New and Improved You*, and *Con-*

fess You're a Mess and Get Clean! are just a few that would attempt to help him. Self-help books only improve an individual's behavior for a short period of time, but they do little to effect long-term change. Jesus didn't come to improve our flesh, but to crucify it, start over, and create something brand new!

I am not condemning Christian books (after all, you're reading mine). If they point to God and His grace as the solution, I am all for them. However, if they simply encourage the reader to try harder in the flesh, they are actually leading that person further away from what God wants for them. Believers need to receive what God has already done for them and learn how to use the gifts He has so graciously given them.

Some of these books put people on a treadmill going nowhere. Temporary victories can be won, but they are short-lived at best. Jesus has given us the solution to overcoming the problems we face in life—and it isn't through our own efforts. Here is the secret: He overcame the world (1 John 5:4). By allowing His resurrected life to live in and through themselves, Christ's followers can find the victory that seems to have eluded them for so long.

In writing to one of the early churches, Paul said, "I have been crucified with Christ and I no longer live, but Christ lives in me. The life I live in the body, I live by faith in the Son of God, who loved me and gave himself for me" (Galatians 2:20). The Christian life is not about trying harder. It is about accepting the fact that believers are "dead," and it is Christ who is living through them. The behavior of a dead person cannot be improved! The resurrected life of Christ within every believer is already perfect, and that life should be lived before a world that desperately needs hope. Christians have the distinct privilege of being the vessel through which God's amazing love and power flows.

Let's get back to the story. Why did Steven howl? Because he thought that he was a wolf, and that is what wolves do. Why does Billy lose? Because somewhere along the way he picked up the perception that he is a loser, and that is what losers do. If Christians focus only on the outward behavior of others, they will never lead people to victory. Instead, they may even drive the lost away. But this is what is happening in churches today where the focus is only on outward behavior. Instead of telling people to quit "howling at the moon" or give up certain habits, believers need to first show them how to receive their true identity in Christ. For the unbelievers, Christians need to show them the way to Christ and then let them know they are not wolves, but beloved children of God, and then they will act accordingly. Even believers need to accept their true identity in Christ before they can have victory in their own lives. Followers of Christ absolutely must stop putting the cart before the horse. When they do, it is very difficult to move!

I am blessed to know many compassionate believers who demonstrate the unconditional love of Jesus each and every day. They emulate Jesus, the One who calls people into their identities with love and compassion. Ironically, Jesus didn't condemn "sinners" for their sin. Instead He showed them grace and mercy. His love changed them.

On the other hand, many well-meaning Christians attempt to "love the sinner and hate the sin." What happens to the person whose identity is completely tied up in his actions? He probably doesn't see the love part, but the hate messages come through loud and clear. What if Steven's parents could communicate to him, "We love you, but we hate wolves"? Steven thought he was a wolf, so he would incorrectly believe that they hated him.

Christians walk a fine and dangerous line when they attempt to love the sinner and hate the sin. Why not just love the sinner and let the Holy Spirit deal with the sin? (Are Christians concerned that others will think they support the sin if they choose to associate with sinners? Wasn't Jesus challenged with the same issues in His day?) It is the job of the Holy Spirit to convict people of their unbelief, and no one else's (John 16:8–9). When the church calls people into who they really are, then the sin is going to fall away. It is God's job—not that of individuals—to deal with sin in the lives of others, and He dealt with everyone's sin quite effectively through the sacrifice of His Son, Jesus. This is the Good News that people need to hear! Many Christians are so busy confronting the world's sins that they lose sight of the lost people who are trapped in sin.

To illustrate this point, I heard a story of a person who was witnessing to people at an abortion clinic. Some Christians were picketing the clinic, and another group of believers was talking to people going in and out of the building and offering them water and snacks. The people picketing were harassing those being kind to the clinic workers and clients for showing them compassion. They were not condoning their actions, but they were showing them love in action. If Jesus were there, I believe He would opt for giving someone a drink of water versus carrying a picket sign. It is His kindness that leads people to repentance (Romans 2:4).

What if Steven's parents had taken him to the pastor, who then proceeded to condemn him for chewing on a bone? Would that have helped him at all? No. Instead of criticizing the boy's actions, Reverend White understood that by first showing Steven who he really was, he would no longer want to chew on a bone! I can almost hear someone say, "So, Michele, you think it's all right for a boy to chew a bone?" As the apostle Paul would have said, "By no means!" (Romans 6:2).

If Christians continually point out people's sins, many will be turned off by the church's message. To the world, many Christians become a bunch of hypocrites who are just spouting off. Romans 8:1 reminds believers that there is no condemnation for those who are in Christ. Jesus did not come to condemn the world but to save it (John 3:16–18). That pure and simple message of grace needs to be proclaimed to a hurting world.

Unfortunately, some people see God as condemning and hateful because that is how they see certain Christians acting. As ambassadors of Christ, believers must represent Him well! (See 2 Corinthians 5:20.)

Christians cannot emulate the world's philosophies when attempting to evoke change in people's lives. The world thinks it will solve individuals' problems by identifying them and labeling them. You are an alcoholic; now stop drinking. You are kleptomaniac; now stop stealing. You are a violent person; now stop beating people up. You are a drug addict, now stop taking drugs. Once individuals receive a negative label, they are doomed to a life of trying not to act out who they see themselves to be. The world's solution is to incarcerate people or medicate them or institutionalize them. This is such a waste of precious life!

The knowledge of humans sadly pales in comparison to the wisdom of God (1 Corinthians 1:20). Praise the Lord as He graciously calls people into their new identities! He gives them a new name, a new heart, and He gives them His desires. It is like the amazing metamorphosis of a butterfly from a caterpillar. The two creatures have absolutely nothing in common in appearance or behavior. A complete and total transformation has occurred. This is what Jesus does for believers. He didn't come to improve them; He came to start over. There is total and absolute victory and freedom in Christ alone!

Although it is important for believers to gather together and have fellowship with one another, I do not believe in Christian pep rallies. These are functions designed to get people all pumped up and committed to stop (fill in the blank with a sin) and start (fill in the blank with a Christian activity). I have been to these rallies and worse yet, I have led them. They do not have positive long-lasting results because they focus on an individual's efforts to attain victory. (Steven, if you commit to trying harder, I know you will stop walking on all fours some day! Just keep trying! You can do it!)

This type of mentality sets people up for failure. A person's flesh will not get any better (John 6:63). God didn't come to improve the flesh, but to crucify it and give believers new life in Him. Trying harder does not lead to victory. Only when someone walks in the Spirit can he deny the desires of the flesh (Galatians 5:16).

Many Christians strive to act more "holy," believing that their holy actions will make them more spiritual. Actually the opposite is true because these are attempts to make the flesh better. When believers realize that in their born-again spirits, they have already been made holy, real change will be manifested in their actions (1 Peter 1:2).

This perfection has been achieved for every child of God in Jesus Christ. Believers receive His perfect Spirit when they accept Him by faith. This is their new identity as children of God. Once they realize who they really are, then holy actions will follow. First horse, then cart.

When I speak to groups about identity, I sometimes have them do an exercise to illustrate the points I have been trying to make. I ask members of the audience to rate themselves as Christians on a scale of one to ten. They are not to share the answers or rate other believers (which might be somewhat entertaining but very disastrous).

Even though people do not share their answers with me, I can guess that most people rate themselves around a five or six, which are fairly neutral numbers—not too boastful and not too condemning. Most Christians judge themselves by what they see in the mirror instead of the way God sees them. This is the "Performance-Based Acceptance Program" that entraps many followers of Christ.

What score would God give believers? Surprisingly, a perfect ten! Why? Because God looks at the hearts of His children, and when He does, He sees Jesus. God scores individuals on

49

the performance of His Son, not on their outward actions. Jesus is a "ten," and 1 John 4:17 states that Christians are like Him in this world! The born-again spirit of believers is the same as that of Jesus because it is His Spirit within them. This is the "Jesus-Based Acceptance Program," which will give absolute victory to every follower of Christ.

People see themselves as a two but want to be a ten. So they try harder in the flesh and fail miserably. Because that doesn't work, they mentally lower their score. Fleshly attempts only lead to pride or condemnation, neither of which comes from God. If people see themselves as God sees them—as a ten—then guess what? They will start acting like a ten. Individuals act like the people they believe themselves to be. Identity influences actions. Actions do not influence identity.

If the cart comes after the horse, it is easy to pull along. The cart will go wherever the horse leads it. Doing it any other way leads to constant frustration. This is where many members of the Body of Christ are struggling today. Jesus has provided the answer for those bogged down with heavy burdens. He said, "Take my yoke upon you and learn from me, for I am gentle and humble in heart, and you will find rest for your souls. For my yoke is easy and my burden is light" (Matthew 11:29–30).

Attempts to improve Steven's behavior without first giving him a revelation of his true identity is a perfect example of cart then horse. However, once he realized who he truly was—a little boy—he began acting like one. When people know who they are, their actions will eventually line up with that truth.

When followers of Christ first receive their true identity as children of God, holy actions will naturally follow as a result. There can be joy and rest in the journey of faith when Christians realize what was already been accomplished on their behalf over 2,000 years ago. Jesus did it all. Hallelujah!

Chapter 5

BEHAVIOR MOD 101

Remember those lessons about behavior modification in psychology class? These are attempts to change behavior based on a system of rewards and punishments. For example, people who are trying to quit smoking may snap themselves with a rubber band every time they want a cigarette. The pain in their wrist is associated with wanting a smoke, and they will not want the cigarette (snap on wrist) any longer. This negative reinforcement is called aversion therapy.

When training animals, people give them rewards for doing the right thing. This is a positive reinforcement form of behavior modification. For instance, if my dog rings the bell before she wants to go outside, I reward her with a treat. Therefore, her actions improve, and she knows what I want her to do as I continue to reinforce her good behavior.

The problem with behavior modification is that it deals with the external not the internal. Anyone can get someone to jump through a hoop, but that person is just going through the motions. It is an external, not an internal change. However, God looks at the heart (1 Samuel 16:7). When Christians want to do something for Him out of love, they have the proper motivation and can accomplish much.

I once heard a story of a woman who lived in a small village. She was working in a field with her newborn baby, who was wrapped in a blanket and lying by her side. Suddenly an eagle swooped down and grabbed the child's blanket, taking it and the child as it soared into the distance. The eagle flew away toward its nest, which was high on a mountaintop. Villagers immediately rushed to the scene and tried to climb the steep mountain to get the child. No one could do it. Strong men and young boys from the village tried in vain to reach the crying child.

Finally, they watched in amazement as a small woman climbed the steep mountainside's rocky ledges to rescue the infant. Why was she able to save the baby when so many people twice her strength failed? Because it was her baby. Love motivates people to do amazing things that go beyond their physical and emotional strength. Love is the greatest motivator of all!

In regard to Steven, the techniques employed by well-meaning therapists did not work. Since the little boy believed he was a wolf in his inner being, his actions demonstrated what he believed to be true about himself. His behavior improved slightly because he wanted food, but he had simply learned to play the game.

How many times do we see people doing the very same thing? Individuals may change their behavior to get the "prize" (a better job, a new love interest, or whatever), but then lapse into their former ways once the reward is obtained. When an issue with a person's actions exists, the behavior is not the only thing that should be addressed. It is a symptom and not the real problem. (That would be like taking several aspirins because someone has a fever instead of addressing the problem or infection causing the high temperature.) God absolutely wants to get to the root of the problem and not just snip off the visible weed. When people don't pull out the roots with the weeds, they always grow back.

In Steven's story, howling and walking on all fours were not his real problem. They were a manifestation of the problem. What was the problem? He thought he was a wolf. He experienced a true identity crisis. Trying to modify only his behavior did not truly help him. I once heard someone say, "Your problem is that you don't know what your problem is, and that is your problem!" This truth applies to Steven's life as he tried to discover his true identity.

The same is true for many people today. Instead of dealing directly with the problem, they treat only the symptoms. Through medication, behavior modification, or other techniques, they try to make themselves feel better. However, true change comes when people recognize their real identity. The challenge is that many people, both young and old, do not even know who they are. That is because they often look to the world to define them instead of to God, the one who created them in the first place.

Environment has a huge impact on the way people see themselves. The majority of the population is raised in the world system with its values and philosophies telling them that only the beautiful, handsome, fit, rich, successful, talented and famous people are important. They receive information about themselves from the media, with very negative results. As a whole, society does not value human life. All of these messages subtly teach people that they have little or no value in the world. When people fall for these lies, they often receive a skewed view of themselves.

One way that people in this world try to modify the behavior of others is through criticism. When I was in college, I had a job that helped pay my way through school. I worked for a boss who was never pleased with anything I did. If I asked a question, I was bothering him. If I decided not to ask, he became upset because I should have consulted him. I could do nothing right!

After working there for a while, I began avoiding the boss altogether. When he came around, I tensed up and wondered what I had done wrong. Since I grew so nervous under his scrutiny, I would make even more mistakes in his presence. Eventually I found another job because I could not handle the constant criticism and demeaning feeling I got from him. He probably believed that by critiquing someone's every move he would get better results from his staff. I don't know of any employees who flourished under this rigid system. Instead of making workers more productive, the criticism made people resentful and angry. The customers we served likely sensed the tension that the employees felt under the critical eye of our boss.

Many people can relate to that situation. They may have had a boss, a teacher, a parent, a spouse, or even a child, who made them feel they could do nothing right. Criticism does not have a long-term positive effect on people. It does not build up; it tears down. Unfortunately some people see God as a heavy-handed taskmaster who waits in heaven ready to zap anyone who gets out of line. (Like me, they would want to avoid "the boss.")

Nothing could be further from the truth since God is love (1 John 4:8). First Corinthians 13, the well-known "love chapter" of the Bible, defines Him perfectly. Verse five says that love (God) "keeps no record of wrongs." So many people believe that He is up in heaven with His clipboard checking off every mistake they make. That isn't God! Let's say that a few days have passed since Steven's revelation of who he truly is. At that point, his mother may get out a clipboard and follow him around day and night keeping track of his mistakes. She would be a very busy woman! Would that help her son? No. It would probably drive him crazy or drive him away from her altogether. (How can a parent help a child when the child avoids him/her completely?) When Steven did make a mistake, what would he need instead of a check mark or demerit? He would need his mother to gently remind him of who he really is. "Steven, remember you're a little boy, and boys don't drink out of the dog dish. Here, have a cup of water." I believe that God also convicts people of righteousness, or their right standing with Him, based on the fact that they are His children. A mind set of righteousness leads to righteous living.

The Lord acts in grace and mercy toward His people. God's judgment for sin was placed on Jesus. By His atoning sacrifice, Christ satisfied the wrath of God for the sins of the world (1 John 2:2). This is the New Covenant in which believers now live (Hebrews 9:15). The Lord not only loves, but also accepts, His children (Romans 15:7). Part of a Christian's identity should be that he is loved and accepted by Almighty God who does not keep track of mistakes. Every critical spirit comes from the enemy, not God.

A Christian's identity should rest in the fact that he is a child of God. Believers have been adopted into His family (Ephesians 1:5) and are, therefore, like Him. If Christians let anyone or anything other than God define them, they will have a distorted view of themselves. How many people in the world are suffering from that very thing? How many people believe they are wolves and yet condemn themselves for howling at the moon?

Young people are especially susceptible to the criticism and influence of others. These negative messages can dog a person throughout his entire life. For example, many students are overwhelmed with peer pressure, and a skewed view of identity can cause a young person to cave in to the pressure, leading to destructive and often life-threatening choices. Furthermore, lowered behavior standards as well as increasing violence in public schools face today's students.

Over my seventeen-year career as a public schoolteacher, I witnessed this firsthand. I will not take the time to discuss all of the possible reasons for this decline since I believe that most people would agree that public schools in general are in a state of turmoil. However, one of the causes for this situation is obvious.

A movement to take God from public schools prevails today. Even though the United States was founded on Christian principles, and students were taught directly from the Bible in the past, the nation is now too politically correct to continue that practice. If taught at all, spiritual matters are from a point of view that discusses all religions as being equal and relevant. Many history books have watered down or eliminated altogether elements of this country's Christian heritage.

A direct correlation exists between removing God from public schools (and the public square in general) and increasing behavior problems and violence within these institutions. By taking Him from the classroom, policy makers have eliminated the very one who defines individuals. They have made it more difficult for students to see His power and purpose for their lives as well as His ability to transform people from something sinful into something holy.

A vibrant knowledge of Jesus gives human beings the realization of good and evil and a desire to be good. Accepting Him as Savior gives them the power to choose good. The ultimate example is Jesus Christ, who demonstrated God's perfect love while He walked the earth. When He is removed from the equation, chaos and confusion ensue. That is obvious in public schools today. Because the solution God provides has been removed, people stand around and scratch their heads trying to figure out how to solve their problems. Many people think that more education is the answer. The philosophy of secular humanism dominates, which basically says that man can eventually solve all of his problems. Please be assured that man is part of the problem— and not the solution!

Educators give mixed messages to kids. These skewed views can negatively impact a person for life. In science class, a child may learn he evolved from primordial ooze. Then he may have some lessons in values that tell him to be honest, responsible and hard-working. If people are all one big accident, then why should they act appropriately? Let's not forget to give a kid a healthy dose of self-esteem. This is the message in a nutshell: *Although you were an accident that resulted from a big bang of some sort, you are really special and should feel good about yourself, be responsible, be kind to others, and don't litter. After all, we should take care of the planet that no one in specific gave us because it would take billions of years for another one to accidentally evolve out of absolutely nothing.* It just makes no sense.

Knowing God created me as a unique and special person gives me a great sense of purpose. It helps me to place myself within the big picture of the world. I have a healthy self-image through the eyes of my Lord who defines me. Recognizing that I belong to Him, and that He made me for a reason, helps me get through this thing called life. Understanding Jesus' sacrifice makes me feel incredibly loved and valuable.

Most people, no matter how young or old, are searching for purpose and meaning in life. They wonder, *Why am I here?*

What is the meaning of life? Who am I? They are looking for love and meaning and want to feel valued. People can only get these virtues from Jesus Christ, the author of life itself. This was the message I so desperately wanted to give my students, many of whom experienced severe crises and dysfunction in their lives. However, as a public school teacher, I could not overtly deliver that message of hope. To know the answer and be prohibited from sharing my faith was incredibly frustrating. I know many Christian teachers who struggle with that very issue every day.

When I wrote about Steven, I made sure that the experts were wrong. People do not need more education; they need revelation of God and His Word. Humans are very limited beings. Nothing is impossible for God, however, and because the resurrected life of Jesus lives on the inside of Christians, they can accomplish anything (Philippians 3:10; 4:13).

Many people in the world are seeking help from a variety of sources. Human beings are often lost, hurting and crying out for help. If I want to diagnose the problem with my car, the best person I can go to is its manufacturer. The same holds true for individuals. If they are truly to get repaired, they must go to the Creator who will not only diagnose, but solve the problem. Jesus is the only hope that this world has.

In the story, the attempts to significantly improve Steven's behavior by using external motivation failed. However, once he recognized who he really was on the inside, his actions lined up quite nicely with that reality. Behavior modification by itself does not work. Knowing one's identity, then living it out, is paramount to true change in a person's actions: "For as he (a little boy) thinks in his heart, so is he" (Proverbs 23:7 NKJV).

Chapter 6

ENEMY TERRITORY

I n the story, Steven was raised in enemy territory. Through an unusual set of circumstances, wolves brought him up as their own, and he mistakenly saw himself as a member of the pack. Because of this, he acted like they did. Many people were raised in enemy territory as well. In saying this, I do not mean that your family is like a bunch of wolves. Although for some of you, that may be entirely true. In reality, most people are raised in the world, a system that goes against the very things of God.

People who grew up in healthy Christian homes where they were taught their worth and identity according to the Word of God should consider themselves blessed. This is not the norm, but it does happen. No home is perfect, and even if someone had the best family in the world, he still may have received some negative messages along the way.

People travel a dangerous path when they begin to blame their own bad circumstances on the actions of others. They use what others have done as a convenient excuse for their own poor behavior. For example, if a woman's parents were verbally abusive, she may in turn say all kinds of hurtful things to her own children. If Mom was an alcoholic, someone may use that as an excuse for why they drink too much. If Dad was physically abusive, his children may in turn abuse others. That is not always the case, but many cycles of abuse continue from one generation to the next. Unfortunately, hurting people hurt others.

When God is invited to be part of a person's life, the destructive cycles of dysfunction can stop. Christians cannot excuse their behavior because of something that happened in the past. There might be reasons that led up to the behavior, but those reasons should not turn into excuses. Believers must acknowledge the offense, forgive those who hurt them, and move on. Unfortunately, people cannot always control what has happened (or is happening) to them, but individuals can decide what they will do about it. Ultimately a person can choose to be a victim or a victor, but the choice is his to make.

I once heard about an interview of identical twins who traveled two very different paths. Their father was an abusive alcoholic. One of the men followed in his father's footsteps, and the other never took a drink of alcohol in his life. The interviewer asked the first brother, "Why do you drink?"

He responded, "Because my father was an alcoholic."

His brother was then asked, "Why is it that you never drank?"

He responded, "Because my father was an alcoholic."

Many types of therapy thrive on excusing a person's behavior because of some event that happened in the past. This does not lead to freedom, but to bondage (not to mention a large bill). If someone wants to be truly free, then God has the answer in His Word.

God says, "The buck stops here." People could blame their parents, and grandparents, and great-grandparents, and so on—but what is the point? It would eventually lead them to Adam and Eve who are ancestors to every person on Earth. That is where sin originated.

I can just imagine Steven lying on a therapist's couch recounting the horror of being raised in a wolf den. If he is not careful, he can let that experience define his entire life. Would there be reasons for his strange behavior? Yes. However, continually making excuses for his actions over a lifetime would be counterproductive. As long as he continued to renew his mind to the truth of his real identity, not the lie that he was a wolf, Steven would find freedom and victory in living out who he truly was. By holding on to past hurts and lies, many individuals are remaining in bondage.

As far as blaming people for the hurt they have inflicted on others, let me say this: People can't give away what they don't have. Let's imagine a young woman named Susan who grew up in enemy territory of her own. Why didn't Susan's parents show her love? Why didn't her parents' parents show them love? Why can't Susan show her children love? Until this woman or anyone else receives love from the one who is love, she won't have it to share it with others. It is that simple. Only people who have received love can give it away. Thankfully, loving people love others.

Some individuals have received a false identity, and have therefore acted out of ignorance. Imagine what would have happened if the wolves had also kidnapped a little girl a year later. Suppose that Steven and the girl eventually had children together. How would they have raised them? As wolves. Their ignorance of the truth would have prevented them from passing on a healthy self-image to their children.

While some people simply do not know better, others act out of willful defiance. They know they are not wolves, but they continue to "walk on all fours" and "howl at the moon." When people willingly choose to ignore truth and act in rebellion, they will then reap what they have sown (Galatians 6:7). Unfortunately, the bad seeds that they sow will often be reaped by others.

The apostle Peter had some harsh words for those who once knew the truth and went back to their old ways: "If they have escaped the corruption of the world by knowing our Lord and Savior Jesus Christ and are again entangled in it and overcome, they are worse off at the end than they were at the beginning. It would have been better for them not to have known the way of righteousness, than to have known it and then to turn their backs on the sacred command that was passed on to them. Of them the proverbs are true: 'A dog returns to its vomit,' and, 'A sow that is washed goes back to her wallowing in the mud'" (2 Peter 2:20–22).

What happens when the dog (or wolf), who is really a person, realizes who he truly is? Absolute victory! Identity in Christ is the key to overcoming the world's temptations and the enemy's lies. When people know who they are in Christ, they won't return to the "vomit" of the past. They need to say, "I'm not a dog, and I'm not a wolf. I have been created in righteousness and true holiness. I need to act like who I am!" The apostle Paul put it this way, "Only let us live up to what we have already attained" (Philippians 3:16). Paul used the word "attained" not "achieved" to show that this identity is a gift, not something people could ever earn on their own!

Part of the lesson in this story is discovering the identity of the real enemy. For Steven, he thought that his parents or other humans were his adversaries. They were the ones keeping him away from his "family." On the other hand, he believed that the wolves were his friends. They were the ones who took care of him, fed him and kept him warm. The wolves also taught Steven to be afraid of people.

Christians can often have a misguided view of their enemy as well. For some, they believe that God is the author of their calamity. They blame Him for the disasters, heartaches and trauma that came into their lives. However, God is good and wants only the very best for His children. John 10:10 sums it up in saying that the enemy comes to steal, kill and destroy, but Jesus came to give abundant life.

It is God's desire that no one perish and all will find the everlasting life He offers through Jesus Christ (2 Peter 3:9). He has provided the way for that to happen, but it is up to individuals to make that personal decision for themselves. He will never supersede a person's will. In their stubbornness, people can often become their own worst enemies as they willfully ignore the hand that God is reaching down them.

Believers can also mistakenly think that another human being is their enemy. Paul writes, "Put on the full armor of God so that you can take your stand against the devil's schemes. For our struggle is not against flesh and blood, but against the rulers, against the authorities, against the powers of this dark world and against the spiritual forces of evil in the heavenly realms" (Ephesians 6:11-12). The true enemy is Satan and his forces of evil. However, God has provided armor to help combat the lies that the devil throws at His children.

One of the most important pieces of armor that God has given believers is the breastplate of righteousness. It protects the heart. Christians should hold up their shield of faith that tells them who they are in Christ. If any fiery arrows should get past the shield, then the breastplate will protect their hearts. When the enemy attacks, individuals can get upset because they sometimes believe the cruel words that were spoken. When believers know who they are in Christ, and that they are right with God through Him, then those darts should not harm them any longer.

I once had someone who continually said some very cruel and hurtful things to me. I grew more and more upset with God because He didn't seem to be doing anything about it. "Are You going to let him talk to Your daughter that way?" I cried out.

God basically said, "You know that breastplate of righteousness I gave you? How about you take it out of the closet, dust it off and put it on?" The key words in this statement are "put on," which meant that I had to receive what God had given me. When I received that gift of righteousness, the words stopped hurting. The arrows could no longer penetrate my heart as long as I had the breastplate of righteousness securely fitted on me.

I finally realized that I had reacted so defensively because deep down inside, I believed the words this person said. This revelation brought so much freedom to my life as I applied it to various situations. God won't shut the mouths of every person who speaks negatively against me, but He has given me armor to protect and defend myself. However, until I put it on, it did me no good whatsoever. Knowing my true identity was a huge step in finding victory and freedom from various attacks of the enemy and his followers.

Once I understood my righteousness in God's sight, everything totally changed. I started to see myself as God saw me, not how the other person viewed me. After this individual quit getting emotional reactions from me, he stopped hurling the arrows in my direction. It is not fun to throw insults at someone who will not engage the accuser. How do you fight fire? With water, not more fire!

God has provided an answer to every problem in His Word. Followers of Christ must use the tools He has given them to fight the enemy and his constant lies and accusations! Some of the most powerful tools a believer can use are the weapons of righteousness that Paul wrote about in 2 Corinthians 6:7. Christians can "fight" the condemnation and accusations with the revelation that they have right standing with God in Christ that comes through faith in Him. If God is for His children, who can be against them (Romans 8:31)?

The devil lurks around looking for someone to destroy (1

Peter 5:8). He was once every person's master, and, like an angry slave owner, he wants people back to serve him. In the story, the wolves were lurking outside the door in the night. They wanted Steven back. The animals did not want the little boy to receive his true identity as a human.

That is how the enemy works. He doesn't want believers to attain the victory that Jesus has already won on their behalf. The devil continues to scream, "You are a wolf! You're one of us! I want you back!" He points out a child of God's every mistake in order to "prove" that he hasn't really changed. This is a battle that many believers face today.

That is why so many people struggle to walk in new life. The enemy is at the window calling them back to their dysfunction. The temptation to return to the old life can be overwhelming, and many people fall victim to the enemy's lies that they cannot change. However, once a believer receives his identity in Christ, the devil has little ammunition to use against him any longer.

The devil has many names: Satan, Father of Lies, The Enemy, The Accuser of the Brethren, and more. Satan loves to get people—even Christians—entrapped in sin, and then use that sin against them. He will beat people down—even Christians—and try to make them feel worthless. The devil will then try to get people—especially Christians—convinced that the things they do define them. He wants to keep believers from receiving their identity as children of God and the victory that comes from that revelation. He doesn't want them to know who their Father is. The enemy loves to keep people in darkness, bondage and suffering. His tool is deception, which can only be countered by the truth in God's Word.

An Old Testament prophet wrote, "My people are destroyed from lack of knowledge" (Hosea 4:6). Another translation states it this way: "My people are being destroyed because they don't know me" (NLT). What don't the people of God know? They don't know God—I mean truly know Him and His loving character. They don't know that He is there to help them in all situations. They don't know who they are in Christ. They don't know what magnificence awaits believers for eternity. They don't know that when God looks at them, He sees Jesus, not their faults. Ignorance of that truth, not negative circumstances, is often the cause of suffering. This truth certainly applied to Steven.

Satan continually lies to people, distracts them, and tries to keep them from the truth about God and who they are in Him. By not truly knowing their identity, Christians allow the enemy to mess with them. They feel they deserve the persecution he sends their way. When followers of Christ are equipped with the knowledge of who and whose they are, they can refuse to put up with the enemy's lies any longer!

One thing the enemy is good at is saying things that condemn believers. "You call yourself a Christian? Look at you. You're a mess. You cannot change. How could God possibly love you?" Some may even think these condemning words come from God. However, Paul writes, "There is now no condemnation for those who are in Christ Jesus" (Romans 8:1). Jesus said that His sheep know Him and recognize His voice (John 10:27 NLT). He is always speaking love and affirmation through His Word and precious Holy Spirit. He is calling people into their true identities and convincing them of their righteousness that comes only by faith in Him (Romans 1:17).

How can believers overcome the temptations to go back to their old ways? They absolutely must renew their minds with the truths that God has given them. If it means shouting, then shout: "I'm not a wolf; I'm a boy! I don't do that any more. That is not what boys do!" The key to victory is to receive identity in Christ and walk in it daily. By renewing their minds to the truths that are found in God's Word, believers can do this. It does not happen overnight, but it does happen. As Christians continue to acknowledge and walk in who they really are, the behaviors and desires of the old self will fall away over time. It is a marathon, not a sprint. Receiving a true identity is a one-time event that happens when someone receives Christ as Savior, but a person must then walk it out or appropriate it in life. Renewing the mind to that reality takes time and effort, but the results are absolutely worth it.

Imagine walking a path in the woods. You walk the same path every day and do so for months. During a bad storm, a tree is knocked down across your path. To make matters worse, there is a large hornets' nest in the downed tree. You decide it is time to take another path.

It is slow going at first. There is not a nice neat path like you once enjoyed. The weeds and briars make walking tough. You may have to take a machete or chainsaw and cut through the underbrush, but you make it through. As difficult as it is at times, you press on. After a few weeks, you notice that your new path has opened up, and it is much easier to walk on it. You also realize that the old path has started to grow over. Weeds and other plants have begun to grow along it so that it becomes harder and harder to see where the original path was.

That is how renewing the mind works. The first time a person has a new thought, the old path doesn't immediately grow over. It takes time to get the new path to become easier to travel. After a while, new habits are formed, and a person won't even think of the old path any more. As Steven might say, "I don't eat out of the dog dish any more; I eat with my family. I cannot believe I ever did that!" At first eating with his family and using a knife and fork seemed awkward, but over time, it became second nature.

Over time, a person will become more and more established in who he really is. For example, the enemy may hold up a picture of a wolf to Steven just shortly after he realized he was really a boy. That visual may cause him great distress, panic, and perhaps reverting back to his old ways. However, what if the devil showed Steven a picture of a wolf after he had a wife, two kids, a dog, a good job and a house with a picket fence? His reaction would probably be thanking God for helping him realize who he really was. That is, after he got done laughing hysterically at the enemy's lame attempt to draw him back into that deception. Being established in your true identity will also help you defeat the enemy in your life as well.

Renewing the mind is not easy. It takes work, and it would be much easier to take a pill, or get wasted, or check out. People will do anything to make the pain go away. Those are the quick and temporary fixes that the world offers, which only lead to more pain, suffering, bondage and destruction. The one behind many of these lies is the devil himself. He uses individuals to do his dirty work and to speak death to broken people. In order to fight against those evil words, a person must take every thought captive to make it obedient to Christ (2 Corinthians 10:5). Counter the negative messages with the Word!

The enemy loves to label people, and then use those labels to keep individuals in bondage. Christians cannot let those negative labels define them. People wear the word "alcoholic" then try not to drink. It doesn't make sense. Instead of labeling himself negatively, a person might say, "I am a child of God who once had a drinking problem, but God gave me a new name!" True victory and freedom come by the renewing of the mind with godly thoughts and with a continuous reminder of the new nature God has given every believer.

A higher power does exist, and His name is Jesus! Alcohol, drugs and other addictions are no problem for Him. With Jesus' life and resurrection power living on the inside of believers, they overcome their problems through Him. When believers are weak, He is strong (2 Corinthians 12:10). Romans 8:37 reminds Christians that in Christ, they are more than conquerors!

In today's culture, it seems like everyone is going into rehab. (Or maybe that is just what the media want people to believe.) It

68

has almost become fashionable. I wonder how effective some of the programs are. If these places are showing people who they are in Christ and helping them receive their true identity, then I applaud them. I know those methods will work. Unfortunately, I don't believe that is usually the case. A lot of people are receiving medication, but what they need is meditation!

When people meditate on the Word of God and what He says about them, their new identities will be manifested through their actions. Most types of therapy deal with the symptoms and not the problem. Having multiple conversations and discussions about the various symptoms of sin helps no one. It is a total waste of time; yet this is where many Christians live.

Individuals need to get to the heart of the problem. Identity is the real issue. If people don't want the weeds to grow back, they need to pull them out by the root. When someone just clips them off, they will grow back with a vengeance. "Oh, you no longer abuse illegal drugs, but now you are addicted to prescription drugs?" Where is the victory in that line of thinking?

If a Christian is struggling with an addiction of some sort, then looking in the mirror with human eyes will do no good. All that person will see is his flaws, shortcomings, wrinkles and failures. When believers see themselves as holy and blameless in His sight, they will come into agreement with what God says about them (Ephesians 1:4). Most Christians want to obey God. One way to do that is to get into agreement with Him. If He says that you are holy and blameless, then believe and receive that! Quit arguing with God, and eventually you will see what He sees. Finally, you will become what He sees. God is the One who calls things that are not as though they are (Romans 4:17). He has called His followers to be holy temples of the precious Holy Spirit (1 Corinthians 6:19). Once that revelation comes, then the addiction will fall away.

If Steven constantly berated himself for being wolf-like, he would probably never achieve victory. However, as he looked into the mirror of God's Word, he could see the potential that resided within him. By constantly renewing his mind to the truth of his real identity, he disarmed the enemy and his arsenal of lies. Light always trumps darkness.

"The reason the Son of God appeared was to destroy the devil's work" (1 John 3:8). God has given believers victory over the evil powers of this world. Jesus has purchased a new identity for those who have received Him. He has given His children armor to protect them from the wiles of the devil. Have you put yours on? Have you been beaten down by the voices, either the current ones or the ones replaying in your memory? Has the enemy told you that you were something you were not? It is time to rebuke those voices and start filling your mind with the voice of God. He is forever telling you that you are special; you are loved; and you are His.

Steven's parents saw what he could be when he was still behaving like an animal. By letting him know his true identity as their child, he could live up to their dreams for him as their son.

Chapter 7

VICTORY

The key to a victorious Christian life is recognizing what God has already done for every believer through grace, receiving it by faith, then acting on it. Believers are not trying to get victory; they are coming from the victory that Christ won for them! The Lord gave Christians a new identity and an inheritance as His children (Romans 8:17). He has done His part. Now it is up to individuals to receive it, renew their minds to this truth, and then live it out.

What if Steven had spent the rest of his life as a wolf after being returned to his human family? He would have been put away in an institution and separated from his family and those who loved him. His parents would have visited periodically and wept at knowing all that had been robbed from their son. What a waste it would be to throw away the potential inside of him! How they would ache for what life could have been for their boy.

The love they had for him would not have changed, but his mother and father would know that he would not achieve all that he had been created to be and to do. I wonder if our Father weeps over all that His own children have become in this fallen world as He sees the wasted potential that lies dormant in so many.

What happened to Steven after the amazing revelation that he was a boy and not a wolf? He began the process of renewing his mind to the truth that he discovered about himself. He may have started to howl at the moon, but then thought, *No, I don't do that any more. I'm not a wolf. I'm a boy, and boys don't howl.* Howling had become a habit based on his incorrect thinking. By renewing his mind to his real identity as a human, he could then live out that identity and break his old patterns and ways of thinking. It is that truth that sets people free. If truth leads to freedom, then error leads to bondage. What is bondage? It quite often involves believing something about yourself that is not true! The story of Steven shows just how destructive and damaging a mistaken identity can be.

Jesus has already achieved the victory for His followers. He tells them who they are as His precious children. That revelation will eventually help them know what to do, but first they need to know who to be. People are human beings, not human doings. Once they learn how to "be," then they will "do."

It is the same with the Christian walk. Believers need to "be" first, then they will naturally "do" as a result of who they already are in Christ. Steven never would have achieved any significant victory by only focusing on his actions. In fact, if he thought, *Someday I will be a human being if I just work a little harder,* he would have lived a lifetime of absolute frustration. However, when he recognized who he already was—his real identity as a human—then his actions followed. First he had to "be," then he could "do."

Many Christians are more focused on the "do" part of their faith than the "be" part. They incorrectly think that God's love has to be earned. Most followers of Christ recognize they are saved by grace through faith (Ephesians 2:8). However, once they are saved, many believe they need to perform for God and earn His love through their own works.

Paul let followers of Christ know how much more, having been reconciled, that they will be saved through the life of Jesus in them (Romans 5:10). Christians are saved by grace, which is a one-time event, and that grace sustains them throughout their entire walk with God. Many Christians speak to sinners about God's amazing grace. However, once saved, some mistakenly believe they need to earn it. This is not what Paul is saying in Romans 5. The Lord desires complete dependence on Him from start to finish. The good works of Christians should flow out of loving obedience to God, not because they want to somehow impress Him or to earn His favor.

I would imagine that Steven's parents loved him just as much when he thought he was a wolf as they did when he realized that he was really their son. However, Steven was able to return that love to his parents once he realized who he was. What joy that would bring his mom and dad as he not only received their love, but gave it back to them! God loves His children unconditionally. He loves those who reject Him, but I believe that God is so pleased when His children receive His love and love Him in return as a result.

God loves His children and wants them to become the people He created them to be. Because Christians are now in Christ, they are "God's workmanship, created in Christ Jesus to do good works, which God prepared in advance" for them to do (Ephesians 2:10). As a result of understanding their identity in Christ, Christians will probably take some sort of positive actions. However, the motivation should be love as they live a life of absolute gratitude for the amazing gifts that God has so graciously lavished upon them.

Christians must learn to walk in the new life that has been given to them. Paul admonished believers by writing, "Do not lie to each other, since you have taken off your old self with its practices and have put on the new self, which is being renewed in knowledge in the image of its Creator" (Colossians 3:9–10). Out with the old, and in with the new! God has provided the "new," but it is each person's job to remove the old and put on the "new" that was a gift of God's grace.

Whenever I write or speak about the unconditional love of God, His grace, or righteousness by faith, I will inevitably get this question: "So does that mean I can just sin all I want to since God loves me anyway?" Paul dealt with this very concern when he preached the message of grace. He wrote, "What shall we say then? Shall we go on sinning so that grace may increase? By no means! We died to sin; how can we live in it any longer?" (Romans 6:1–2). Sin is a very serious issue, and I do not want to make light of it. Sin destroys lives, kills people, and creates a multitude of problems in the world. God didn't wink at sin or turn His back on it. Sin separated man from God, and God sent His son to the cross to take away sin and reconcile man to Himself. Praise God that Jesus dealt with sin once and for all (Hebrews 10:10).

I would like to take the liberty of rephrasing Paul's question. "What shall we say then? If Steven's parents love him no matter what, then why can't he just continue to live as a wolf and do whatever he wants?" When the question is posed that way, I believe it sheds light on what Paul was trying to say. Steven's parents loved him, but they wanted more for him than growling at his siblings and eating out of the dog dish. They saw him acting like something he was not, and it grieved them terribly. Yes, they loved him apart from his behavior, but to let him remain in that state without some type of intervention would be an atrocity.

God loves His children. Like any good parent, He wants the very best for His kids. The Lord wants them to live to their full potential and to become who they were truly created to be in righteousness and true holiness. Anything less than that would be an absolute tragedy! God sent His Son in order to reconcile people to Himself. Humans were designed to have a relationship with God, and they can through Jesus Christ. To know (experience) God is eternal life (John 17:3). It is much more than just going to heaven and avoiding hell, but intimacy with the Creator in a meaningful and powerful way on a daily basis. Eternal life is available now!

What if Steven recognized he was human but decided to stay as he was? What if he didn't let the reality of his identity influence his actions? That would have been an incredible waste! To ignore one's God-given abilities and potential is a terrible thing; yet it happens all the time. When I see people who struggle with addictions or live a life of absolute dysfunction and depravity, my heart cries out. I want to shout, "Don't you know who you could be? You were created in the image of Almighty God, and He loves you! He has so much more for you than this!"

The mission of every Christian should be to call people into their true identities. They should be convincing the lost of righteousness instead of judging them. Believers should never say, "Stop walking around on all fours! Why are you eating out of the dog dish? What is the matter with you?" Those messages of condemnation help no one.

This is one of the main reasons the church as a whole has failed to give out the message of God's unconditional love and grace. Instead of showing the compassion of Christ, too many reflect the judgment and condemnation like the Pharisees of Jesus' day. Then people complain that no one wants to come to church. Romans 2:4 reminds Christians that it is God's kindness that leads people to repentance. God's kindness!

There is a disturbing movement in this country to come against things of Christ. From defaming the name of Jesus in movies and television shows to taking the words "under God" out of the pledge to our flag, the nation's Christian heritage is being challenged. Just over fifty years ago, people were outraged that evolution was being taught in schools. Now people are persecuted for teaching creation. It is troubling to see how fast things have changed in such a short time.

Many factors have caused this shift. Because the United States is a "melting pot" for the world, it has let the world influence it instead of influencing the world. The children of Israel faced the same situation on their journey to the Promised Land. God chose them and set them apart from other nations. The Lord made them His holy people, "his treasured possession" (Deuteronomy 14:2). Throughout their travels, they let other nations negatively influence them with deadly consequences. It led to idolatry and worshiping false gods.

Sadly, the same thing happens to believers today. Peter writes, "But you are a chosen people, a royal priesthood, a holy nation, a people belonging to God, that you may declare the praises of him who called you out of darkness into his wonderful light" (1 Peter 2:9). The chosen people that Peter referred to are Christians. Instead of declaring God's praises for calling them out of darkness, many are busy trying to point out the sins and problems of the world. Therefore, Christians have brought some of the persecution that they face on themselves.

I once heard a disturbing testimony from a new believer in Christ. She had been an abortion activist and at one time led a destructive lifestyle. The young woman testified that she became a follower of Christ despite some of the Christians she met. How incredibly sad is that?

Jesus did not carry picket signs or boycott anyone or sign petitions. He did not point out people's sins and condemn them. He compassionately spoke life to the lost, one individual at a time. He valued them and showed them their worth. When the lost encountered the Lord, His love changed them. If Christians are not showing love, even to the unlovely, they are simply a "clanging cymbal" and not part of the symphony of love God wants them to give to the lost. Without love they are nothing (1 Corinthians 13:1–2).

When Christians point out other people's sins, then fall themselves, they look like a bunch of hypocrites to the world. It also sets them up for scrutiny if they make a mistake. On the other hand, a believer can perform 9,999 acts of kindness, but fall one time, and what gets reported? Not the acts of kindness, but the mistake. I am not supporting or condoning the error; however, the media love to broadcast the sins of Christians. This gives the world a skewed view of God's people when only their errors are put on public display. This is part of the world's system, which loves to focus on the negative and also thrives when people mess up. When a Christian gives grace after another person falls down, hopefully he will receive grace when he falls down.

As a whole, followers of Christ must take a new approach to reaching sinners with the message of the gospel. They need to be saying, "This is not who you really are. You were created to be a child of God. Look in the mirror. Can you see that you look like your Father? God loves you and wants the very best for you. Receive your new identity in Christ! It is a gift you could never earn, but God wants to give it to you free of charge simply because He loves you." I am blessed to know many believers who share this message of God's unconditional love with others each and every day. They inspire me.

What about you? Have you received your new identity in Christ? If not, what is holding you back? Do old habits and negative ways of thinking have a grip on you? How successful have you been in breaking free of those? You may have found that any success is temporary because it was based on your efforts instead of what God did on your behalf.

When you grit your teeth and try harder, you will often find that those increased efforts only lead to further guilt and condemnation when you fail. It is a cycle that I call the hamster wheel. It goes something like this: conviction brings on increased effort, which leads to some success followed by pride and then a fall. Then comes the guilt, condemnation and promises to try harder next time. Then a person increases his effort, and the cycle begins again. Hamsters exert tremendous amounts of energy yet go absolutely nowhere! People either spend their entire lives on the hamster wheel and achieve no victory whatsoever, or they simply quit the race and give into the temptations that hound them. Sound familiar?

God wants you to live up to your full potential. He wants you to become everything you were created to be (Ephesians 2:10). In order to begin that journey, you must first receive what He has for you. If you have never received Jesus Christ as your personal Savior, this would be a fantastic time to do that. You simply receive the gift of salvation and eternal life by faith. You believe it and accept it for yourself. You do not have to clean yourself up to come to God. He loves and accepts you just as you are; however, He will help you overcome the challenges that plague you in life because He loves you.

Once you accept Christ, the Holy Spirit comes to live inside you. Your spiritual identity is transformed instantly. Your father is no longer Adam, but Jesus. This changes your spiritual DNA. Because you have been born again, God no longer sees you as a sinner, but as a saint instead. Remember that identity is determined by birth, not actions. By grace, God has done His part. Now it is time for you to access it by faith. By then renewing your mind with God's Word, you will be transformed from the inside out.

It is time to take back your identity like Steven did. Like him, you have just looked in the mirror and said, "I'm a child of God, and I look like my Father." For a moment, take your eyes off your performance and look to Jesus, the one who performed for you. He is able. He is faithful. He is worthy. Now enjoy the amazing journey of discovering who and whose you are. You will never be the same.

If you already are a Christian, then celebrate and rejoice in all that God has done for you. Jesus defeated sin and death on the cross, and this is the victory that Christians celebrate. Believers are more than conquerors in Him (Romans 8:37). My prayer for you is that grace and peace will be yours in abundance as you get to know Jesus more and more (2 Peter 1:2). I also pray that you will let God's light within you shine before all people, and that you will be prepared to give a reason for the hope that you have in the Lord (1 Peter 3:15). This is what the lost need in their lives. Jesus, living inside you, is the answer to someone's prayers. I pray that God will give you opportunities to share His love in the name of Jesus. I imagine Him rejoicing as you become all He created you to be.

Chapter 8

SINFUL NATURE

What if Steven spent his entire life with "two natures" warring inside of him? He would have lived in a state of constant conflict and confusion as he tried to figure out who he truly was. Perhaps he would determine whether he was a wolf or a boy by his actions at any given moment. If he spent a lot of time licking his "paws," well then, in his mind he was a wolf. But when he interacted positively with his siblings in a game of checkers, he saw himself as a boy.

The wolf nature was an illusion based on his ignorance of truth. The enemy had deceived him, and he bought into it until someone broke through his wall of deception. As long as Steven let his actions determine his identity, he would have no real victory in his life, and he would always be confused about who he really was.

Many Christians experience the same kind of struggle. They mistakenly believe that there is a war going on within them. In this line of thinking, when they exhibit holy actions, then they are saints. But after committing a sin, they wrongly believe they are sinners, when the old man, the sinful nature, rears its ugly head.

What happened to the old man or sinful nature? It was crucified on the cross with Christ so that the body of sin could be done away with (Romans 6:6). In Galatians 2:20 Paul reminds believers that they were crucified with Christ, and it is not they who live but Christ who lives in them. What part of believers was crucified? The sinful nature. Those who have died (spiritually reborn individuals) have been freed from sin (Romans 6:7). Let's put it this way: How possible is it for a dead man to have a sinful nature or sin as a result?

The enemy does not have to defeat Christians. He can get them to defeat themselves. A double-minded individual is unstable in all he does (James 1:8). If people think they have two natures warring against each other within them, they may eventually implode, and Satan can just stand back and watch them blow up. One of the enemy's most destructive tactics is to divide and conquer whether it be among people or within individuals.

Why do so many believers continue to struggle with sin? One reason is that they rely on feelings more than on God's Word. I have already established that feelings do not always line up with truth. People may feel that the sinful nature is alive and well, but the Word says it no longer exists. Christians must stand on God's Word above all else—especially their feelings!

Another reason many struggle is that Christians are to walk by faith, not be sight (2 Corinthians 5:7). Unfortunately, this does not always happen. When people look in the mirror, they may see all of their flaws, both internal and external. However, when individuals are born again, it is their spirit that comes to life. They still look and often act the same, but a true transformation did take place in their innermost being.

The prophet Ezekiel foretold of this event when he wrote, "I will give them an undivided heart and put a new spirit in them; I will remove from them their heart of stone and give them a heart of flesh" (Ezekiel 11:19). A physical change does not occur, and since so many people walk by sight, they don't realize that something incredible has changed within them. A heart transplant is not visible to the naked eye!

People see their mistakes and weaknesses with human eyes; however, God looks at them through rose-colored glasses. In other words, He sees His children through the blood of Jesus. For Christians, a big part of obeying God is to believe what He says about them and to walk by faith, not by sight or feelings.

The enemy would love for Christians to believe that the sin nature is alive and well. This is often how he gets them to do his dirty work. He often approaches them and speaks to them in first person. A former drug addict may think, *I want to take drugs*. Satan disguises himself as the old sinful nature so that it seems like it is still alive. This is why so many believers fall back into old habits and can never seem to get complete victory over their old ways.

In order to help build his case that the old self is still alive and kicking, Satan will accuse believers of everything they have done wrong. (If you want to receive the freedom that comes from knowing your true identity, you might want to brace yourself for this attack by equipping yourself with the armor described in Ephesians 6:11–18.) The enemy wants those who once followed him and his lies to continue to live a life of bondage when in reality, they have been set free by Jesus Christ (Galatians 5:1).

There is a war going on, but it is not an internal one. The war is between the kingdoms of light and darkness. As soldiers in the Kingdom of light, Christians must be equipped with the knowledge of who they are as they prepare for battle. The enemy wants them to feel like the sorriest, most wretched, worthless sinners on the face of the planet. Believers then spend more time beating themselves up than attacking the real enemy!

I know of Christians who do nothing but berate themselves and apologize for how pathetic they are. (I used to be one of them.) Then they take this defeated attitude into battle and get their clocks cleaned! I cannot emphasize enough the importance of knowing who and whose you are! God is for you, so who can be against you? (Romans 8:31) The enemy has no authority to bring any charges against God's elect (Romans 8:33).

Romans 5 through 8 are vital chapters in understanding the gospel of grace. In chapter 5, Paul wrote about Jesus dying on the cross for people while they were still sinners, and that believers are justified by faith in Him. In chapter 6, Paul told followers of Christ that their sinful natures were crucified on the cross, and they should consider themselves dead to sin and alive in Christ. In chapter 7, Paul illustrated the battle that can go on in the mind of a person who thinks that there is a war going on within them. (Note the number of "I" statements in this chapter. This leads to defeat!) Finally, chapter 8 illustrates how victory has already been achieved in Christ when Christians live their lives through the Spirit. "The mind of sinful man is death, but the mind controlled by the Spirit is life and peace" (Romans 8:7). Romans 8 is one of the most encouraging chapters in the entire Bible! (Whenever I get discouraged, I always go back to it.)

The apostle Paul knew who he was and to whom he belonged. He did not operate from his past. If he did, then he would have constantly berated himself for persecuting and murdering followers of Christ. This was the old Paul (Saul), but Jesus changed him and gave him a new name and new identity. With this security, he was able to boldly proclaim the truths about Jesus the Messiah to the very people he once persecuted violently. I have no doubt that the enemy tried to resurrect the old man in order to keep Paul from the battlefield. Praise God that Paul would have nothing of it!

Before I understood my own identity in Christ as a new creation, I took Satan's bait. He served up a platter of my worst sins, faults and shortcomings, and I ate it up. For many years I tried to be a better Christian and attempted to get my flesh to act more holy. It only ended up in frustration and defeat. In fact, it almost caused me to quit the race altogether.

Once I learned that the person I kept apologizing for no longer existed, I was set free. An amazing thing happened during that time. Instead of using my freedom to sin, which Paul warned against in Galatians 5:13, my actions became "holier" more by accident than they ever did on purpose. My relationship with God flourished as I let Him lavish His unconditional love and acceptance on me. I became the person He created me to be when I quit trying and started trusting.

Second Peter 1:4 states that believers are participants in the divine nature. Does God have two natures? Of course not. Believers who have been born anew in Him do not have two natures either. The enemy has created an illusion of a second or sinful nature, and those lies can only be destroyed by the truth of God's Word. First John 5:18 states, "We know that anyone born of God does not continue to sin; the one who was born of God keeps him safe, and the evil one cannot harm him." When armed with the sword of the Spirit (the Word of God), the enemy cannot harm you either.

Most Christians do not want to sin, but they feel that with their old sinful nature, they are powerless over sin. They make statements like, "I'm only human. I'm a wretched sinner. I can't help it. I'll never change." Then they continue to live a lie by operating from the old man. The devil will try to resurrect the old you, but you must remind him that he/she is dead. Dead people don't sin, and they cannot be tempted!

Religion has turned the grace of God into something that has to be earned. Most believers have heard many sermons preached about not sinning. How effective are those messages? Some well-meaning ministers give sermons that attempt to get Christians to try harder. Many people in the body of Christ think the answer to their problems is through more self-effort. It puts them on a hamster wheel going nowhere, but they sure exert a lot of energy and waste precious time.

What if a person tries really hard and overcomes a sin? He may feel prideful, which is not of God (James 4:6). What if a person tries really hard and falls into temptation? Then condemnation will result, which again, is not of God (Romans 8:1). So how do Christians achieve victory over sin? By trusting that Jesus living in and through them will not sin and by recognizing that the sinful nature has been crucified on the cross.

Jesus is the only one who overcame sin in the first place! Getting the flesh all fired up not to sin leads people nowhere fast. The Spirit gives life, but the flesh counts for nothing (John 6:63). This is the message that both Christians and non-Christians alike need to hear!

Not wanting to sin is a noble goal. What should believers do when the enemy impersonates that old man? Remind Satan that the old man is dead, that he no longer exists; and praise God that He made them new creations in Christ (2 Corinthians 5:17). This is the new and true nature of every child of God. This is the real you created to be like God in righteousness and true holiness (Ephesians 4:24)! This is a faith not a flesh issue. Followers of Christ must renew their minds to this reality.

Once Steven fully realized he was a boy, he probably felt pretty silly about his wolf-like behaviors. He might even have compared himself to his siblings or other kids his age. What if he could have communicated this message to his mother: "I am a mess. I don't know how to walk, or talk, or do other things that people do. I can't even use the bathroom like other people do! Once I get that all figured out, then I will be worthy to have a relationship with you. When I get things straightened out, I will contact you, then we can build our relationship"?

His mother would hear nothing of it! She had been robbed of enough time with her boy, and she wouldn't want to waste another second while he "got his act together." Steven saw his sin; his mom saw her son. Nothing could separate him from her love, including his actions. Yet how many times do individuals deal with God in the same way? They falsely believe they have to clean themselves up to come to Him. This could not be further from the truth. He wants a relationship with people now, and He is not interested in waiting until they shape up. It will never happen!

What if God never saw your sin? What if you could approach Him any time with no thoughts of what you have or have not done? What if you could come boldly before Him knowing that you were completely loved, forgiven and accepted? What if you were holy and blameless in His sight, and He simply delighted Himself in you and your uniqueness? What if you could trade in your sin for His righteousness? What if He just loved spending time with you? What if your relationship was solely based on His perfect work on your behalf and had nothing to do with your efforts or performance?

Well, I can tell you that all of these "what-ifs" are true. How would you respond to this kind of love and acceptance? By sinning all you wanted to because it didn't matter? I doubt it. People respond to love with love. You would be able to fulfill the greatest commandment which is to love God with all your heart, mind, soul and strength (Mark 12:30). To me, that means loving Him totally with your spirit, soul and body.

An amazing thing will then happen. Once you have received that perfect love, you will be able to love yourself with a healthy God kind of love. This is a huge gift from the Father and one that not many unwrap. (How many people wallow in self-hatred because they see nothing but their flaws, faults, sins, mistakes and regrets?)

Finally, once individuals receive love and love themselves as a part of God's unique and beautiful creation, then and only then can they love their neighbors. This is what God wants for His people. This is what God wants for you.

Paul told believers how to attain (not achieve) victory (Philippians 3:16). He admonished them to walk by the Spirit in order to deny the desires of the sinful nature or flesh (Galatians 5:16). What does it mean to walk in the Spirit? It means to get into agreement with God and His Word. It means to walk by faith in the finished work of the cross. Paul also warned followers of Christ that their performance and self-effort would cause Jesus to be of no value to them (Galatians 5:2–6). Ironically, self-effort does more damage to a person's relationship with Christ than anything else.

Steven did not have two natures. The war within himself was based on false information that he received in enemy territory. The only difference between Steven and believers is that the boy was never a wolf in the first place. Prior to being born again, people did have a sinful nature as a result of the Fall. They sinned as a result. When someone receives Christ as Savior, he is born again. The old things have gone, and the new has come (2 Corinthians 5:17).

The old man with the sinful nature is dead and buried. It is time to stop trying to dig him up and resuscitate him. You have been set free to be the person whom God created you to be, and you are free to love God, yourself and others. The Lord has given you a new nature. He is the one who gives life to the dead and who calls things that are not as though they were (Romans 4:17).

If the Son has set you free—and He has—you are free indeed (John 8:36). You can now live a life of thanksgiving and love for Jesus Christ, the one who did it all for you.

Chapter 9

RULES AND REGULATIONS

Before Steven realized he was not a wolf, he probably would have needed a list of rules to help control his behavior. It might have looked something like this:

1. Don't howl at the moon.
2. Don't eliminate waste on the carpet.
3. Don't eat out of the dog dish.
4. Don't bite your sister.
5. Don't growl or snarl.
6. Don't "mark your territory."
7. Don't crawl on all fours.
8. Don't chew up the couch cushions.
9. Don't chew on bones.
10. Don't eat out of the trash can.

As long as Steven believed he was a wolf, he would need a very long list of do's and don'ts to get him in line. Would that have turned him into a "person" in his mind? Probably not. What good are rules when people don't know who they are?

God gave a set of rules to His own children as well. The Law or Ten Commandments were given to the people of Israel through Moses. His job was to lead between two and three million people, who were once held in bondage, to the Promised Land. During that journey, God gave the commandments, which were written on stone tablets (Exodus 20). For a very long time, the Law has been a controversial subject for the church. In order to help clarify some misunderstandings about it, let's look at commonly asked questions pertaining to the Law and its relevance for believers today.

What was the purpose of the Law? Under the Old Covenant, God gave rules or laws to His chosen people to keep them in line. God loved His people, or He would not have taken them out of slavery. Like any loving parent, God provided rules in order to help His children. The fallen world was full of lawlessness and rebellion as a result of man's sinful nature, which was alive and well before the cross. God had to make rules because of the transgressions of the people, and it was put in place until the Seed (Christ) would come (Galatians 3:19).

Through the death and resurrection of Jesus, the Law was fulfilled. The sinful nature of believers was crucified on the cross, thus the Law became obsolete in their lives (Hebrews 8:13). Paul states that Christ is the end of the Law so that righteousness would come to everyone who believes (Romans 10:4). The Law was never intended to make people right with God. Righteousness has always come by faith alone (Romans 4:3, 13).

If the Law doesn't help make people right with God, why was it given? The Law was designed to help people see their total need for God; it was never intended to be something for believers to follow in the age of grace in which they now live (Galatians 3:19). The Law is a mirror to show an individual that his face is dirty, but that same mirror cannot clean it. The Law is impossible for anyone to fulfill except for Jesus Christ. He did not come to destroy the Law, but to fulfill it. Love is the fulfillment of the Law (Romans 13:10).

Is there anything wrong with the Law? No, the Law is holy (Romans 7:12). God created it, and everything that He creates is good. The problem was not with the Law but with man (Hebrews 8:8). Because of man's sinful nature, the Law actually stirred up sin instead of restraining it (Romans 7:5). Telling a person not to do something makes him want to do it all the more. However, without the Law, there is no consciousness of sin (Romans 3:20). God had to show people the difference between wrong and right. Through the Law, God continued to draw people to their need for Him.

Let me ask the same question this way: Is there anything wrong with a hammer? A hammer is neither good nor bad. It is a tool that can be very helpful if used correctly.

The key is how people use the hammer, or in the previous case, the Law. Both are tools which can be used for harm or for good. It is of utmost importance to understand how to use these tools properly to get the best results. Many people are driven away from God because the "hammer" has been used to beat them up instead of pointing them to the Lord Jesus.

Can the Law keep people from sinning? The following statement is crucial for believers to understand in order to have a victorious Christian walk: Preaching the Law actually arouses sin; it doesn't prevent it (Romans 7:5).

Here is an illustration of that point: Right now, as you are reading this book, I don't want you to think about a red car. Please, I beg you: Do not let a red car enter your mind. I implore you; stop thinking about the red car no matter what!

It is easy to see what happens. The very fact that I keep mentioning the red car, which was not on your mind initially, is suddenly front and center. All that you are thinking about is red car, red car, red car. The world would label you a "red car thinker," then try to help you by telling you to quit thinking about the red car. Years of therapy and large bills would follow until you finally would "overcome" your problem. I hope you can see the futility in this line of thinking.

What if I told you instead, "I don't care if you think of a red car or not, but let me tell you about the amazing God that I serve. He designed the heavens and the earth. God has shown us what infinity looks like as space goes on forever. He created those stars you see in the sky, and He is making more right at this moment. He also formed the tiniest speck of life here on Earth. God designed the world and all of the life in it from the smallest insect and tiniest hummingbird to the enormous blue whale and elephant.

"Above all, He created people in His image. That's right; you are made in the image of God! He made everything good, but man let sin into the world through his disobedience. But wait! God provided an answer through His Son, Jesus Christ. Through Him everything is held together (Colossians 1:17). God knows all about you, and He loves you. The Lord has an amazing plan for your life. He wants to make Himself known to you as He reveals His endless love. By inviting Him into your life, you will embark on an unforgettable journey that is truly life-changing. And when this life is over, He has made a way for you to spend eternity with Him in heaven! What an awesome God we serve!" Guess what you forgot to think about? Beep, beep!

What about "good" people? Do they need the Law? Basically the Law was designed to shut the mouths of people who thought they were good (Romans 3:19). In the world today, individuals will compare themselves among themselves (2 Corinthians 10:12). They might think, Well, I'm not as bad as so and so. At least I never killed anyone.

God sets very high standards, so high that no one could possibly follow them except Jesus. In addition to the Ten Commandments, there were also more than 600 other laws that were added to the Law by people. James 2:10 states that if a person breaks one law, it is as if he has broken them all. (That makes over 600 broken laws for every person. Ouch!) The commandments were designed so people would see their sin and turn to Jesus for the forgiveness that He purchased for them on the cross.

What if someone keeps most of the Law? Is that good enough? People might be satisfied with a passing grade. But with God, it is all or nothing. In His sight, 99% is failing. Jesus told His followers that if a person is angry with his brother, it is as if he killed him (Matthew 5:22). He went on to say that a man who looks at a woman with lust in his heart has committed adultery with her in God's sight (Matthew 5:28). Man looks at the outward appearance, but God looks at the heart (1 Samuel 16:7). Jesus was talking heart issues in His sermons. God had to raise the bar so high that no one, not even the best high jumper in the world, would try to leap over it. Unfortunately, many people still believe that it is possible to fulfill the Law on their own. God has made it very clear that it cannot be done. He wants people to trust completely in the finished work of Jesus on their behalf.

Why would God give His people a set of rules that they could not follow? The only one to fulfill the Law completely and perfectly was Jesus Christ. It was designed to point people to their absolute need for a savior. God does not want His people to try to obtain righteousness through obeying the Law, but through faith in Christ alone (Romans 3:21–22). The bottom line is this: Jesus + Something = Nothing. Jesus + Nothing = Everything. This is the grace in which believers must stand. They must acknowledge that Jesus did the job that He was sent to do with 100% accuracy and finality. It is time to accept and celebrate this amazing truth!

Is the Law for Christians today? The Law is good if one uses it properly (1 Timothy 1:8). If a person thinks that he can enter heaven by being "good," then the Law can help him see that there is no way he can ever be good enough to enter heaven without faith in Christ. The next verse states that the Law is made for lawbreakers and rebels, the ungodly and sinful, but not for the righteous (1 Timothy 1:9).

By now I hope you realize that righteousness comes only by faith, not by an individual's performance or by following the Law (Philippians 3:9). Therefore, the Law is not applicable to believers who live in the age of grace today.

How is the Law used improperly? The Law does have a purpose, but it is used in the wrong way when people try to be justified by it. Paul warned believers that those who are trying to be justified by the Law have been alienated from Christ and have fallen away from grace (Galatians 5:4). He went on to say that the only thing that matters is faith that expresses itself through love (Galatians 5:6).

Finally, believers who are led by the Spirit are not under the Law (Galatians 5:18). This describes a point of maturity in Christ. When Steven matured as a person, he would no longer need the "law" or rules of his parents. His identity would define him and dictate his actions, and the rules would no longer be necessary.

Imagine Steven in his mid-thirties with a wife, children, home, dog, good job, and so on. What if someone approached him with his list of rules and reminded him not to soil the carpets any more or bite his little sister? Giving him those old commands would be offensive. (They might even stir up sin, and his wife would not like that.) Again, once he is established in his true identity, a long list of rules would be unnecessary. Once he had built relationships with people, his motivation would be love, not following a list of rules.

What if people under the New Covenant try to follow the Law? Most Christians want to be good and do the right thing. There is nothing wrong with trying to obey the commandments.

94

Believers should not steal, commit adultery, put idols before God, and so on.

However, it is important to understand the motivation behind following the Law. Is a person relying on the Law to be justified by following it? If so, that person has placed himself under a curse (Galatians 3:10). By trying to follow the Law, an individual sets himself up for failure because all of the commandments needed to be followed perfectly, without any error whatsoever, in order to obtain right standing with God. This is what people faced under the Old Covenant. Of course, this was absolutely impossible for anyone to accomplish except Jesus. Those who put their trust in Him have fulfilled the Law and its requirements. Jesus fulfilled it for them.

Here is a good way of looking at this subject: When you are under the Law, you have to obey it. When you live under grace, you want to obey. Obedience comes from a loving relationship not a list of rules. "This is love for God: to obey his commands" (1 John 5:3). Believers love first, then obey as a result of that love. God places His holy desires in the hearts of His children, and they desire to please Him. And what is the only way to please God? By faith (Hebrews 11:6). The Law is not based on faith (Galatians 3:12).

What about the laws of Christ? Should believers follow them? God said, "This is the covenant I will make with the house of Israel after that time ... I will put my law in their minds and write it on their hearts" (Jeremiah 31:33).

What are Christ's laws? They are to "love the Lord your God with all your heart and with all your soul and with all your mind ... (and) love your neighbor as yourself. All the Law and Prophets hang on these two commandments" (Matthew 22:37–40). When you love someone, you don't want to harm them in any way. When you love God, you don't want to put anything before Him. When you love yourself, you take care of the temple God gave you. Yes, Christians should joyfully follow the laws of Christ that have been written on their hearts. By His grace, Christ gives them the power and desire to do so.

First John 5:3 says that God's commands are not burdensome. Would fulfilling over 600 laws perfectly be a burden? Absolutely! However, John was not referring to the Law here. He wrote about following the laws of Christ. Believers are to operate in the love that comes from the Father to them and then through them. Love should never be a burden because it flows from God to Christians to the world.

Why haven't so many Christians fallen in love with God and placed Him above everything else? Perhaps because people are too busy trying to earn His love as opposed to simply receiving it. That is nothing but pride, which God strongly opposes (James 4:6). Why don't many people love their neighbors? Because they first have to love themselves. When Christians walk in love and grace, they are able to give love and grace! The following illustration might help explain this concept:

Imagine you are on an airplane flying someplace warm and tropical. Suddenly the plane malfunctions, and you find yourself and the other survivors swimming for your lives in the ocean. Thankfully, everyone survives and there just so happens to be a deserted island just 100 yards from the crash site. People swim to safety and discover their new home.

Now let's imagine that the passengers on the plane had been complete strangers. Tempers flare, and people quickly begin to dislike each other. Each hoards what few resources he has, and many became violent. In order to survive in the new community with limited food, water and supplies, a few leaders arise from the group to take charge. They come up with a set of rules and regulations in order to avoid chaos and anarchy on the tiny island. The list grows and grows. As long as the people on the island continue to live in strife, there also has to be a plan to punish those who choose not to abide by the rules. Certain individuals might even be banished from the group if they do not cooperate.

On the other hand, let's say that your plane crashes with people from your church. The entire plane is filled with members of your congregation. You are headed to a third-world country for a mission trip when the plane goes down. Since you are all believers, you operate in complete unity and love while submitting to each other. Everyone puts the needs of others before himself. (Hey, it's my story, and I can write whatever I want!)

Since you all walk in love, you don't need a lengthy list of rules in order to maintain a sense of peace and stability on the island. As long as you love God, yourself and others, you all live in harmony as you cheerfully share what you have with others until the rescuers came to save you. Love supersedes the rules!

Another reason that many people have not fallen in love with God is because they do not truly know Him and His goodness. Throughout my Christian walk, I have discovered that most people treat others as they see God treating them. In other words, if I see a person who is very judgmental, that person likely believes that God is judging him. When I observe a person who is critical, I assume that the individual incorrectly thinks that God is criticizing him. Instead of being transformed by the true nature of God, many turn into the image of the "god" whom they perceive.

Why is the Law so controversial within the body of Christ? I wish I had the answer to that question, but I do have some theories. First, following the Law can become tradition—and tradition, although comfortable, can negate the work of God (Mark 7:13).

Secondly, pride has a lot to do with it. Many people believe they can follow the Law. The flesh always wants to do something, to perform and to impress. A person who thinks he can follow the Law without fault is like an individual who believes he can high-jump to the moon. It is laughable, yet many try to accomplish the impossible.

Third, I believe that the Law can be used to try to control and manipulate people. This can come from the head of a household or the head of a church.

Most importantly, I believe that many people use the Law as a way to help control their own behavior. If it were removed, what would prevent them from sinning? Some Christians do not understand that they have the laws of Christ written on their hearts, which will cause them to operate in love as they lose the desire to sin. Also, part of the fruit of the spirit is self-control (Galatians 5:22–23). This fruit will naturally be produced as Christians abide in Christ (John 15:1–17).

To illustrate this point, I am reminded of a story about workers building a bridge many years ago. The people paying to have it built did not want to go to the added expense of placing a large safety net below the workers. They believed that installing a net underneath the men would cause the workers to goof around, fall into the net on purpose, and therefore not get a lot of work accomplished.

The bridge builders had to work at high elevations above the roaring waters of the river below. After a time, they got used to it and maneuvered around the steel beams with little thought of the crashing waves underneath them. That is, until one of the workers fell to his death in the icy waters below the job site.

When work on the bridge resumed, the men were petrified and got very little done. Each step and every maneuver was slowly and carefully calculated until the builders were accomplishing almost nothing. Once someone was killed, everything came to a standstill.

The people in charge of the bridge finally put a net in place. To their surprise, work resumed, and the men got the bridge done in record time. Only a few people accidentally fell into the safety net, and when they did, they quickly got right back to work without much thought.

The net represents grace. It catches believers when they fall, helps them to get back up, and saves them from certain death. Once the church has a complete revelation of God's grace, it too will cause the body of Christ to accomplish more than it ever did when it was under the Law. The Law paralyzes and produces fear while grace sets people free: free to love and serve God in appreciation for all that He has done for them through Christ.

If Steven's parents only imposed rules on their son, he would eventually form a skewed view of his mother and father. They may have initially needed some rules in order to set boundaries before a relationship could be developed, but rules do not deal with heart issues. This old adage is true: Rules and regulations without relationship lead to rebellion.

When Steven thought he was a wolf, he probably had a distorted way of defining his parents. He likely saw them as enemies trying to keep him from freedom. When he finally understood that he was their son, he could then develop a healthy view of them over time and eventually come to know and love them. The same holds true with God and His children today.

The resounding message in this book proclaims that God should define His creation. People must receive their identity from Him, and then appropriate actions will naturally follow as a result of that revelation.

However, there is a disturbing movement in the world today for the creation to define the Creator. There is a huge difference between discovering who God is and trying to invent Him. While this may sound educated and open-minded on the surface, a careful examination of this philosophy reveals that it is blasphemy. Taken to an extreme, some say that many paths exist to God which the Bible clearly contradicts.

People who uphold the "many paths" doctrine are treading in extremely dangerous waters with eternal consequences. The Bible clearly states that Jesus, God's one and only Son, is the only way to the Father (John 14:6).

To say there are many paths to God is an overt slap in the face to the Lord Jesus. It is proclaiming Jesus to be a liar, which is absolutely not the case. To claim that another way to God exists is to say that Jesus suffered excruciating pain, agony and humiliation on the cross for nothing. With this way of thinking, other "gods" could have accomplished the same thing.

If there are indeed many paths, world religions would be aligned instead of contradicting each other. The words of Christ ring true when He said, "Enter through the narrow gate. For wide is the gate and broad is the road that leads to destruction, and many enter through it. But small is the gate and narrow the road that leads to life, and only a few find it" (Matthew 7:13–14). Those who accept everything, in reality, believe nothing.

It seems as though many people are confused and tired of religion. Religion is defined as man's attempts to reach up to God by following rules and trying to earn righteousness based on one's own ability. Christianity is considered a world religion, but by definition, it is not religion at all.

The difference between Christianity and all of the other religions in the world can be summed up in one word: grace. Religion tries to earn its way up, but grace flows down from the Creator to the creation.

Jesus came against the religious philosophies of His day. He rebuked the Pharisees, the ones who thought that they were made right by following the Law; yet Jesus showed compassion toward sinners. Many people lump Christianity along with other world religions because they don't see the difference. Because so much conflict among religions occurs today, people often throw the baby out with the bathwater. That baby is Jesus.

Religion tries to get people to perform for God. Grace demonstrates how God performed for the world through His Son, Jesus Christ. Believers are no longer under the Law (Romans 6:14). Christians should now live by faith in the Son of God, who loved them and gave His life for them (Galatians 2:20). They are to walk in love (2 John 6). When they do, they will have no desire to harm their neighbor, or to covet what he has, or to slander him in any way. When they understand the true nature of God as their provider, they would have no need to steal.

When people fall in love with God as a result of all He has done in and through them, they should no longer have a desire to put false gods before Him. Now that the New Covenant has been established in Christ, the Old Covenant is obsolete (Hebrews 8:13). The Law served its purpose and was fulfilled by Jesus.

Rules and regulations are turning people off and causing them to rebel. What so many people are desperately seeking is a real relationship with their Maker, which is what God created humans for in the first place. That can come only through faith in Christ.

The Law was intended to help people realize their need for God. Unfortunately, the devil has once again twisted God's Word and deceived many people. The enemy has made individuals think they need to follow the Law in order to be right with God. He uses the Law as a hammer with which to hit people over the head and to bring condemnation and defeat to God's people.

Attempts to follow the Law lead to frustration, defeat, and perhaps turning from God altogether. The Law is a ministry of death (2 Corinthians 3:7). Trying to follow it to be right with God puts people under a curse. (Plus, it cannot be done in the first place.) The devil holds people ransom and uses the letter of the Law as blackmail.

When used properly, the Law should point people to their need for a savior who is Jesus Christ. When used improperly, the Law can drive people away or negate the work of Jesus in a person's life. He fulfilled the Law for believers, and this is the good news that needs to be proclaimed boldly throughout the world.

Christ gives His followers their new identity as His children. In return, they love Him and others. Like Steven, when children mature and realize who they are, they no longer need laws or rules to guide them. The message of love is written on their hearts.

When Anna and Kevin faced losing their son all over again, they went to a pastor for help. He didn't give the boy rules and regulations to follow, but a revelation of who he truly was from Almighty God. This saved Steven's life.

Chapter 10

TRUE FREEDOM

So many people do not have a good understanding of what freedom really is. Some believe that being free is doing whatever they feel like doing. That is not freedom; it is bondage. Others may think that living a "free" life means having one big party and really living it up. Many of those activities lead to bondage and addictions, which are certainly not freeing at all.

So what is freedom? In part, it lies in knowing one's identity then acting on it. In the story, Steven found freedom when he came to an understanding that he was not a wolf, but a human being. That revelation put him on a path to true self-discovery. He could live out who he already was, a little boy. This realization would eventually lead to a change in his actions. But the cart could not come before the horse. First he had to know who he really was; then his actions would follow and change over time. The bottom line is this: An individual will act like the person he believes himself to be.

There is a big difference between "free" and "freed." The best illustration for this truth comes from history. When Abraham Lincoln signed the Emancipation Proclamation, he freed all slaves. Were all slaves free? No. Some owners did not inform slaves of their freedom. Many slaves were kept in the dark so their masters could continue to use and abuse them for personal gain. All of the slaves were freed, but only some were truly free. How horrible would it be for a slave to learn that he had been freed years before, but because of his ignorance of that truth, he remained in bondage unnecessarily?

Jesus came to set the captives free (Isaiah 61:1-9). Who were the captives that Scripture was talking about? Every person on Earth. When He shed His blood on the cross and died for the sins of the world, then rose again, He freed the entire world from sin. Is everyone free? No, but they have all been freed by Jesus Christ. This message of freedom needs to be proclaimed from the rooftops!

God has provided freedom, but it cost Him a lot. He gave up His Son so others could enjoy it. Freedom of any kind is never free. There is always a price to pay, and praise God, Jesus paid the ultimate price for sinners. He gave up His very life on the cross, and His motivation was love for people and for God. Jesus said that the knowledge of truth will set individuals free (John 8:32). Praise God that He paid for everyone's freedom in full! However, ignorance of that truth is keeping many in bondage today.

If knowledge of truth leads to freedom, then error often leads to bondage. One of the biggest errors I see in the Christian church today is the belief that saved people are sinners. This is absolutely a case of mistaken identity. I often hear the phrase "sinner saved by grace" and there is no such thing. Christians were once sinners, and they have been saved by grace, but there is no Scripture which points to a believer being a sinner. A look at two verses Paul wrote will help explain:

"When we were still powerless, Christ died for the ungodly" (Romans 5:6). "While we were still sinners, Christ died for us" (Romans 5:8). If those verses are lined up, they are virtually the same. The words "powerless" and "sinners" are almost interchangeable. How much power did Steven have to change his behavior when he thought he was a wolf? Basically none. He was helpless because he didn't know his identity. He was a victim of the lie he believed about himself. Once the revelation came, the power, motivation and determination followed. This is an amazing truth that also applies to the lives of Christians today.

When believers were yet sinners, they too were powerless to change their actions. Oh, but how some have tried! Followers of Christ should recognize that God dealt with the sin issue through Jesus. He gave them a new name or identity. However, many may still be trying to manage their sins themselves in futile attempts to please God. Does accepting their new nature as saints mean that believers don't sin? No. But their identity was changed from sinners to saints when they received Christ. This is an identity issue, not a behavioral one.

Many people think that in order to stop being a sinner, they need to quit sinning. However, that will never happen! People will make mistakes until the day they die, whether they want to or not.

In Romans 14:23, Paul says that anything that does not come from faith is sin. Sin is what a person does that he knows is wrong; it is also neglecting to do something that he knows is right. Does every Christian walk in faith 24/7? No. As people mature in Christ, they walk in faith more and more, but no one reaches perfection in this life. Believers have perfection (the Holy Spirit) living on the inside of them, but the flesh will never get better. Recognizing that reality should move Christians to stop trying to improve their flesh. It is an exercise in futility!

Remember that the Christian life is not a changed life but an exchanged life. People who are born-again are new creations in Christ; "the old has gone and the new has come!" (2 Corinthians 5:17). Christians are sealed with the Holy Spirit (Ephesians 4:30). Saying that a person is a sinner saved by grace is kind of like saying that a butterfly is a flying worm. It just doesn't work that way.

I once attended a Christian event with nearly one thousand other people. A prominent female athlete prepared to deliver a message to the group. She enthusiastically shouted, "Good morning, saints of God!" I think about ten people responded. Now what if that same woman would have walked in and said, "Good morning, all of you wretched sinners"? I bet most people would have clapped and hollered. That is a sad but true reality within the body of Christ today. Many Christians love to condemn themselves, but those in Christ face no condemnation (Romans 8:1). Aren't believers "in Christ"?

The apostle Paul addressed believers as saints. He did not base that label on the things they had done because many of these people were not acting in a "saintly" manner. In fact, many of them were committing very vile acts, which Paul addressed in his letters. He called people saints based on the finished work of Jesus on their behalf. They were believers, and therefore, they were saints. His message could be summed up this way: "Jesus died for you, and you have received this message by faith. That makes you saints. Now start acting like who you really are!"

Understanding the difference between saint and sinner is crucial in a Christian's victorious life. This revelation brings true freedom. Remember the verse that says, "For as he (a man) thinks in his heart, so is he" (Proverbs 23:7 NKJV). If a person receives the label "sinner," what will the resulting behavior be? That's right, sin. The most natural thing in the world for a sinner to do is to sin.

If people receive their righteousness by faith and not by works, then they are saints! When they believe themselves to be saints, what kind of actions will naturally follow? That's right, holy ones. The same thing happened to Steven. He received his identity as a boy not a wolf; then he started acting like a human. A person's actions do not change his identity, but a person's identity will influence his actions.

Many Christians do not feel good unless they feel bad. Receiving the name "saint" is too uncomfortable for them. They rattle off more sins than you can shake a stick at and conclude with, "Well, how can I be a saint when I do this and this and that? I'm just an old wretched sinner."

Did howling make Steven a wolf? No. Does sinning make someone a sinner? No! An individual's identity was changed to a saint when he received Jesus. Praise the Lord!

Many Christians will tell me they are sinners saved by grace. To that I respond that if they are truly saved, they're saints. The Bible says that sinners should be banished from the earth and the wicked no more (Psalm 104:35). A "hellfire and brimstone" message like that can send believers into a panic. They will try to "quit sinning" in order to avoid hell.

Again, believers are not sinners. This term refers to people who reject the free gift of salvation Jesus has provided. It's not about what Christians have done, but it is about what Jesus has done for them. The enemy is very good at convincing believers to try to earn what they already have. Simply put, it wastes their time so they are not out proclaiming the good news of God's grace. They think, *Once I quit sinning, then I will go be a witness.* Well, you will never be a witness with that attitude, and that is precisely what the enemy wants.

In 1 Timothy 1:16, Paul referred to himself as the worst of sinners. Some may argue that if Paul was calling himself a sinner, then that is what believers still are. In this group of verses, Paul was describing himself prior to his conversion. In other words, before he believed in Jesus as Lord, he was the chief of sinners. If Paul was such a wretched sinner, then he must have been "drinking, cussing, chewing and going with girls who do"—right? No, Paul called himself a sinner as he attempted to follow the letter of the Law. His most wretched sin was that of self-righteousness and unbelief in Jesus as God's Son. He wrote about the ways in which he persecuted the church violently and had Christians murdered for putting their faith in Christ (Philippians 3:6).

Paul admittedly acted in ignorance and unbelief and was shown mercy by God (1 Timothy 1:13). Once his eyes were opened to the truth, he used the same zeal that he once used to persecute the church to witness to the church and cause it to grow. Paul was a saint, not because of his saintly actions, but due to his born-again experience and encounter with the risen Lord. His new identity then influenced his actions, which involved laying down his life for the cause of Christ. Paul considered everything he had once prized so dearly to be rubbish as compared to the infinite value of knowing Jesus Christ as Lord (Philippians 3:8).

Paul understood the importance of being free in Christ and realized there were people around him who did not want others to enjoy their newfound freedom. In Galatians 2:4, he wrote about the false brothers who infiltrated their ranks to spy on the freedom that Paul and his fellow believers had in Christ. What was Paul free from? The Law—the very thing he once considered of great value as he obeyed it without fault (Philippians 3:6–7).

The Law drove him to persecute the church and even stone Christians to death. People can become very radical and violent while trying to obey rules and follow laws even in the name of religion. This is quite prevalent in the world today.

Freedom is one of the most misunderstood concepts in the world today. Most people think that freedom means being free to sin. In reality, it means having the freedom to love and serve God as a result of no longer being under the Law, which brought a curse if it was not followed precisely (Galatians 3:10). Knowing that believers do not have to perform for God will bring glorious freedom and joy! Paul reminded Christians of the importance of being free many times throughout the book of Galatians. However, he emphasized that believers should not use that freedom to satisfy the flesh but instead to serve one another in love (Galatians 5:13).

The entire book of Galatians is one of Paul's masterpieces because it warns believers (past and present) of the dangers of mingling the Law and grace. Perhaps his strongest words come in Galatians 5:4 where he says, "You who are trying to be justified by law have been alienated from Christ; you have fallen away from grace." Do you want to be alienated from Christ or have Him be of no value to you (Galatians 5:2)?

I say this to warn you of the dangers of mixing the Law and grace in your life. Also, beware of those who will try to enslave you by making you follow the Law instead of encouraging you to live by grace. Romans 6:14 says, "For sin shall not be your master, because you are not under law, but under grace." (Remember the Law stirs up sin. Red car, red car, red car!)

If the Law could make individuals right with God, then Jesus died for nothing (Galatians 2:21). Unfortunately, the issues that Paul faced nearly 2,000 years ago are still prevalent in the church today. Once people taste true freedom, they will never want to be put in bondage again!

Some people believe that the grace message is only an excuse to sin. I admit that I once thought that myself. However, a close examination of the life of the apostle Paul counters that misconception. Paul preached freedom from the Law. Did he use it as an excuse to sin or to lie around and do nothing? No. He beat his body and made it a slave as he fervently preached the gospel to the Gentiles (1 Corinthians 9:27). He endured horrific persecution unto death. Even when Paul was in prison or facing death for the sake of Jesus, he was free.

Paul wrote many of his letters from prison. Why was he in jail? For preaching that Jesus fulfilled the Law and that righteousness came by faith in Christ alone. The same people who sent Jesus to the cross did not like Paul proclaiming the message that believers no longer needed the Law as their guardian since Christ had come (Galatians 3:25). The irony is that Paul used to be one of them as he fervently persecuted the church. The Lord had hand-picked Paul for the specific task of reaching the Gentiles (Galatians 1:15–16). People praised God for this amazing transformation in his life (Galatians 1:24).

Believers were once slaves to sin, and are now slaves to righteousness (Romans 6:18). Understanding these powerful truths is crucial to a victorious Christian life. Even though a person reads these words on the page and even looks up various Scripture references, it takes a revelation from Almighty God to understand these truths. Have you received God's revelation about freedom in Christ? I pray that you have.

Many people remain in bondage as they struggle with their identity. They see themselves as sinners, but they don't want to sin. People receive a negative label and then try to act differently. There is no victory here. The most natural thing for a wolf to do is to howl. The most natural thing for a sinner to do is sin. When believers receive their true identity in Christ as saints of God, they will become the people they believe themselves to be. It may not "feel" right, but believers must be determined to walk by faith and not feelings.

God calls "things that are not as though they were" (Romans 4:17). A perfect example of this truth is a man named Gideon. He was weak and the least in his family, yet what did the angel of the Lord call him? A mighty warrior (Judges 6:12–15). Once he received that label, what did he act like? That's right: a mighty warrior!

When God calls His children saints, it is hard to believe. But if God said it, His followers should not argue with Him. In Romans 14:23, Paul reminds believers that anything not of faith is sin. Calling yourself a sinner if you are saved is not of faith! People who see themselves as sinners will produce sinful behavior. Those who are truly sinners can instantly become saints by being born-again. The saint/sinner issue needs to be understood by the church as a whole. Its members must put on the robe of righteousness that God has given them in Christ! It is through faith that the righteous have life (Galatians 3:11).

At one point in his life, Steven probably felt comfortable with the "wolf" label. He exhibited wolf-like behaviors, so in his mind, he was an animal. However, his feelings did not match up with his true identity. His father might have proclaimed, "Behold my beloved son, Steven. Some day he is going to be a mighty man of God. The Lord and I have great plans for him!" That statement would have made the boy feel strange and uncomfortable as he looked at himself with his own eyes. His father, however, knew something that Steven didn't. Kevin knew what was truly inside of his son, and he found a way to bring that God-given potential into fruition. The revelation of his true identity gave Steven the freedom to be all he was born to be.

When believers receive who they are by faith, their actions will follow. Followers of Christ are free to love God and to serve Him with all of their hearts. The scriptures declare that everyone was once a prisoner of sin, and God's promise of freedom comes only by believing in Jesus Christ (Galatians 3:22). "If the Son sets you free, you will be free indeed" (John 8:36). When people see you enjoying your newfound freedom in Christ while passionately loving and serving Him, they will want what you have. Freedom, victory and peace will draw a crowd!

Chapter 11

REFLECTIONS

I recently told the story *Wolf Boy* to a group of people who had suffered terrible bondage because of abuse and addictions throughout their lives. I could only guess the countless times they had been wounded in life. My heart ached when I thought of all they had suffered either by their own hand or someone else's. I wept when I heard the sad tales of the many consequences they endured as a result of the negative circumstances and choices in their lives. I was especially saddened to hear of families separated and children taken from their parents. To know that innocent lives suffer in this fallen world is especially hard to bear.

I wondered if these people had families who loved them and if they had ever been shown their worth in life. Did they know who they really were and all they could be? The world had certainly beaten them down. But praise the Lord, they were in a place of healing where loving Christians were feeding them the Word of God and helping them recover. This was a place of new beginnings.

As I looked at these wounded people, I could only imagine the countless ways in which they had tried to seek help. They had probably heard multiple messages that told them to "straighten up and fly right." That message was completely ineffective. They didn't know how to fly at all. When people receive Christ, He gives them wings. He teaches believers how to fly and calls them to soar high and free. Oh what freedom and joy there is in Jesus Christ!

As I talked to this group about what happened to Steven, many in the audience cried throughout the entire story. One young woman sat in the corner with her arms wrapped tightly around her waist as she rocked back and forth. I heard her keep whispering to herself, "I'm not a wolf. I'm not a wolf." Another stepped outside and looked to the sky and wept cleansing tears of joy. I saw radiance on her face as she looked at the sun. Praise God for this amazing revelation that can only come as the Holy Spirit bears witness to the fact that they are His righteous children, destined for glory.

After I left that day, I spent a long time thinking about the experience and meditating on *Wolf Boy*. I knew that the people in this rehabilitative program would soon leave to go back home. I sensed the fear of those who were preparing to return to the environment from which they had come. Would the temptations that used to plague them lure these individuals back into dysfunction and addiction again?

I realized more than ever that a person absolutely must have a strong sense of identity in Christ before going back into the "world." If those individuals in the treatment center knew who they truly were, they could partake in the victory that was already won for them over 2,000 years ago in a place called Calvary. Trying to get the flesh under control wouldn't work, but walking in the Spirit and knowing their identity as children of God would lead them into the abundant life Jesus promised (John 10:10). After all, an individual will act out the person he believes himself to be. Butterflies have no business crawling on the ground like worms. When they do, it is easy to trample them.

God gave me a powerful revelation as I reflected on this entire experience. He said, "Do you know why you acted like a fool all those years? You thought you were a wolf." Wow, all of those times I had beaten myself up for walking on all fours, what was I thinking?

I had believed a lie about myself and then acted in absolute ignorance and unbelief. My behavior then reflected it. I was living out the person that I mistakenly thought myself to be. In saying this, I am not trying to excuse my mistakes, but I do better understand why they happened. This revelation has also freed me to forgive myself and others who have harmed me along the way.

These truths help me appreciate my real identity and freedom in Christ all the more. It also gives me a strong sense of responsibility to continue proclaiming this message and thank God for giving me opportunities to share it with people who still believe they are wolves. This is the ministry of reconciliation that God has given to all of His followers (2 Corinthians 5:18).

The world thinks that if it punishes people and points out all of their mistakes, they will shape up. It thinks that if it puts labels on people and medicates them enough and counsels them enough, they will improve. Its philosophy is to point out all the negative aspects of individuals and hope they will change for the better.

This type of condemnation only reinforces what they already believe to be true about themselves. How many so-called wolves are sitting in our prisons today? How many are institutionalized or hospitalized with no apparent hope? How many have been medicated to the point of addiction? God provides hope and restoration and healing. He calls those things that are not as though they are. He reaffirms who people are in Him, even when they don't feel close to Him. The world cannot offer hope to the lost because it doesn't have the answer. That answer is Jesus Christ and His gospel of grace.

The gospel is good news. In fact, it is great news! One would think that every person on Earth would jump for joy at hearing it. Unfortunately, that is not the case. There is one group of people that does not want to receive this message. Who would that be? Those who are self-righteous. They think they don't need the righteousness of Jesus that comes by faith alone because they are already "good" in their own minds. They follow the rules and are proud of their efforts. James 4:6 is a good reminder that God opposes the proud but gives grace to the humble. Sad to say, these people are often very religious.

The same was true in the day of Jesus. The religious folks of the day, the Pharisees, did not want to hear that right standing with God was a gift that only came through faith in Christ. Jesus spoke His harshest words to the Pharisees. He called them hypocrites and white-washed tombs who looked good on the outside but were evil on the inside (Matthew 23:27–29). What did they do in return? They demanded that Jesus be crucified in a horrific way.

The good news is for people who see their need and humbly receive by faith what God has for them through His amazing grace. Paul warned people to examine themselves to see whether or not they were in the faith (2 Corinthians 13:5). That is something that individuals need to do. After receiving Christ, every person has an opportunity to come boldly before the throne of grace to receive mercy in his time of need (Hebrews 4:16).

Jesus promised a full life for His followers. Understanding one's identity in Christ opens the door to that abundance of grace. All too often people are defined by what happens to them instead of by who they are. For example, Steven would have been known as the "wolf boy" to people who had heard his story. If he let that terminology define him, he would have stayed in bondage his entire life to the circumstances he had endured as a child.

Many people allow the hurtful things that have transpired in their lives to define them, and it becomes hard to break free from that past. (For example, a person might have gone through a divorce, but wearing—accepting—the label "divorcee" becomes negative and demeaning.) When people immerse themselves in their identity as children of God, the baggage from their former lives gets lost along the way. The things that happen in life become events, not ways to define individuals. When God defines His children, then new life truly occurs, and the old labels and ways fade away.

What about you? Have you humbled yourself before the Lord? Have you received your identity in Christ as a precious child of God? What is your story? Have you been raised in enemy territory, and for the first time are you beginning to see who you really are?

Have you achieved a success in life, and now that it is gone, you long for the glory days to redefine you? Have you been wounded by the church or religion, and now you want nothing to do with God? Has this world given you a label that you are trying to shake, but you can't seem to break free? Have you been verbally abused, and those negative voices keep playing in your mind over and over?

Have you been physically hurt by people who were supposed to love you? Have you been unfairly judged or discriminated against over something you cannot control? Have you been abandoned, rejected or ignored? Are you so consumed with regret over past mistakes that you cannot forgive yourself? Have you taken your pain and inflicted it on someone else?

Have you abused your body with drugs and alcohol in an effort to numb the pain that won't seem to go away?

Did you let this world define what success and beauty are? Are you a perfectionist who believes you have to perform perfectly in order for someone to love you? Who has lied to you? Let God deal with those individuals, and keep walking in the new identity that you have received.

Jesus Christ can heal the broken places in your life. He came to destroy the works of the devil (1 John 3:8). He is the only one who can do that for you. He will let you know who and whose you are. He can show you your value and purpose. Above all, He will love you unconditionally, and never leave you or forsake you (Hebrews 13:5).

Each and every human being is a precious creation of Almighty God. Let the Potter define you. Let Him then mold you and shape you into exactly what He created you to be. When you have been shaped by the Master's hand, your life will never be the same. You cannot change where you have been, but you can change where you are going! Praise God for this awesome truth.

Give your mistakes and regrets to Jesus. Joel 2:25 says that God will restore the years the locusts have eaten. In other words, He will pay back what the wolves in your life have stolen. You are not one of them. You are a child of the King. He will define you and give you an inheritance that you cannot comprehend. He will whisper in your ear, "My precious child, you belong to Me, and no one will snatch you from My hand" (John 10:29). Receive your identity from Him and live out who you were created to be. Above all, receive your wings, and fly!

Look in the mirror. Can you see the person that God made in righteousness and true holiness? Whisper to yourself, "I'm not a wolf. I'm a child of the Most High. I am His." When that truth soaks deep into your heart, it will change you from the inside out. It is time to walk upright, my friend.

When I wrote the story *Wolf Boy*, I chose the name Steven randomly—or so I thought. I began to wonder what the name meant, and I discovered its meaning is "crowned one." That is a beautiful picture of Jesus crowning His sons and daughters with their identity as children of the King. It is time to receive your crown as well.

"Praise the LORD, O my soul; all my inmost being, praise his holy name. Praise the LORD, O my soul, and forget not all his benefits—who forgives all your sins and heals all your diseases, who redeems your life from the pit and crowns you with love and compassion, who satisfies your desires with good things so that your youth is renewed like the eagle's. The LORD works righteousness and justice for all the oppressed" (Psalm 103:1–6).

I would like to close with Paul's prayer in Philemon 6. "I pray that you may be active in sharing your faith, so that you will have a full understanding of every good thing we have in Christ." May Jesus be glorified and magnified in your life. He makes all things new.

ABOUT THE AUTHOR

Michele Eich lives in the Quad City area of Illinois with her husband Lynn. Together they have six wonderful and energetic children. Michele taught in the public school system for seventeen years before leaving the classroom to pursue her dream of writing and speaking about the amazing ways in which God has worked in her life. She is a graduate of Charis Bible College and the founder of Finally Free Ministry, which emphasizes God's unconditional love and freedom in Christ. Michele is passionate about the Word of God and its ability to set people free to become everything that God created them to be. To contact Michele, please visit www.finallyfreeministry.com.

IDENTITY VERSES

These verses describe the new you. This is who you are in your born-again spirit. By renewing your mind to these truths, you will become the person that God created you to be. Receive your new identity in Christ, and holy actions will follow!

John 15:1, 5	I am part of the true vine.
John 15:15	I am a friend of Christ.
John 15:16	I am chosen by Christ to bear fruit.
Romans 3:24	I have been redeemed and justified.
Romans 5:1	I have been justified (completely forgiven and made righteous) through faith. I am at peace with God.
Romans 6:1–6	I died with Christ and to the power of sin's rule over me.
Romans 6:7	I have been freed from sin's power in my ife.
Romans 6:18	I am now a slave of righteousness.
Romans 6:22	I am enslaved to God; He is my gentle Master.
Romans 8:1	I am forever free from condemnation in Christ.
Romans 8:14–15	I am a son/daughter of Almighty God.
Romans 8:16	I am a child of God.
Romans 8:17	I am an heir of God and co-heir with Christ.
Romans 11:16	I am holy.
Romans 12:2	When I renew my mind in God's Word, I know who I really am.
Romans 15:7	Christ has accepted me based on His work, not mine.
1 Corinthians 1:2	I have been sanctified (set apart).
1 Corinthians 1:30	God placed me in Christ, who is now my wisdom from God, my righteousness, my sanctification and my redemption.
1 Corinthians 2:12	I have received the Spirit of God into my life so that I would know the things given to me by God.
1 Corinthians 2:16	I have the mind of Christ.
1 Corinthians 3:16	I am a temple of God; His Spirit lives in me.
1 Corinthians 6:17	I am one with the Lord in spirit.

1 Corinthians 6:19–20	I have been bought with a price, and I am not my own because I belong to God.
1 Corinthians 12:27	I am a member of the body of Christ.
2 Corinthians 1:21	I have been anointed by God.
2 Corinthians 2:14	God always leads me in His triumph in Jesus.
2 Corinthians 5:14–15	Because I have died, I live for Christ, not for myself.
2 Corinthians 5:17	I am a new creation in Christ; the old is gone, the new has come.
2 Corinthians 5:18–19	Because I have been reconciled to God, I am now a minister of reconciliation.
2 Corinthians 5:21	I am the righteousness of God in Christ.
Galatians 2:4	I have freedom in Jesus Christ.
Galatians 2:20	I have been crucified with Christ. I no longer live, but Christ lives in me. The life I live is through Christ by faith.
Galatians 3:26	I am a child of God.
Galatians 3:28	We are all one in Christ.
Galatians 4:6–7	I am a child of God and an heir through Jesus.
Ephesians 1:1	I am a saint.
Ephesians 1:3	I have been blessed with every spiritual blessing in Christ.
Ephesians 1:4	I was chosen in Christ before the foundation of the world to be holy and blameless before Him.
Ephesians 1:7–8	I have been redeemed and forgiven, and am a recipient of His amazing grace.
Ephesians 2:5	I have been made alive with Christ.
Ephesians 2:6	I have been seated with Christ in heaven.
Ephesians 2:10	I am God's workmanship, created in Christ to do His work that He planned for me to do.
Ephesians 2:13	I have been brought near to God through the blood of Christ.
Ephesians 2:18	Jesus gives me access to the Father by one Spirit.
Ephesians 2:19	I am a fellow citizen with the saints and a member of God's family.
Ephesians 3:6	I am a fellow heir, a fellow member of the body, and I share in the promises of God through Christ Jesus.
Ephesians 3:12	I may approach God boldly and with confidence.
Ephesians 4:24	I am righteous and holy.
Philippians 3:20	I am a citizen of heaven.

Philippians 4:7	God's peace guards my heart and my mind in Christ Jesus.
Philippians 4:19	God will supply all my needs according to His riches in Christ.
Colossians 1:13	I have been delivered from the domain of darkness and transferred to the Kingdom of light.
Colossians 1:14	I have been forgiven of all my sins. The debt against me has been cancelled.
Colossians 1:27	Christ dwells in me.
Colossians 2:7	I have been firmly rooted in Christ and am now being built up in Him.
Colossians 2:10	I have been made complete in Jesus Christ.
Colossians 2:11	I have been spiritually renewed. My old nature has been taken away.
Colossians 2:12–13	I have been buried, raised and made alive with Jesus. I am totally forgiven.
Colossians 3:1	I have been raised to new and resurrected life in Christ.
Colossians 3:3	My life is now hidden with Christ.
Colossians 3:4	Jesus Christ is my life.
Colossians 3:12	I am chosen of God, holy and completely loved.
1 Thessalonians 5:5	I am a child of light, not of darkness.
2 Timothy 1:7	I have been given a spirit of power, of love and of self-discipline.
2 Timothy 1:9	I have been saved by grace through faith and called according to God's purpose.
Hebrews 3:1	I am a holy brother (sister) with a heavenly calling.
Hebrews 4:16	I may come boldly before the throne of God to receive mercy and find grace in my time of need.
1 Peter 2:9–10	I am part of a royal priesthood and a holy nation, a people who belong to God.
1 Peter 2:11	I am an alien and stranger to this world.
1 Peter 5:8	The devil is my enemy. He is my adversary, but I have victory over him in Christ.
2 Peter 1:4	I have been given His precious and magnificent promises. I am a partaker of His divine nature.
1 John 3:1	God has bestowed His great love on me and calls me His daughter/son.

QUESTIONS FOR DISCUSSION

Chapter 1 – Steven

1. Have you ever heard of a feral child? If so, take some time to discuss what you know about this phenomenon. If time allows, do a little research on the subject. Some of the real life stories are shocking.

2. What do you think of the prognosis of the so-called experts?

3. Have you ever faced a situation where you consulted the "experts" before you consulted God? How did that work for you?

4. Think of an example of a time when God took you through a situation and solved your problem in a powerful way. Write about or share those times.

5. Look up Joel 2:25–26. How do these verses apply to this story?

Chapter 2 – Identity Theft

1. Who or what most defines you?
a. What I think about myself
b. What others say about me
c. The world's definition of who I should be
d. What God says about me in His Word

2. If you answered a, b or c, then you may have an identity crisis. Choose five scriptures from the "Identity Verses" section and write each down on an index card. Place them where you will see them daily. This is how you will begin to renew your mind to what God says about you.

3. What are some of the labels you have received in your life? Have they been constructive or destructive?

4. Why is knowing your identity in Christ so important?

5. Write down ten things that describe you. Then cross off the things on your list that could change tomorrow. What does this exercise tell you about yourself?

Chapter 3 – Split Personality?

1. Why do so many Christians struggle with their feelings?

2. Has the spirit, soul and body teaching helped you in your Christian walk? If so, how?

3. Why is Romans 12:2 important for believers to understand and apply to their lives?

4. Did Steven's feelings line up with truth? Apply this to your life and discuss or journal your answer.

5. What part of you should be in total control (spirit, soul or body)? Explain.

Chapter 4 – Horse and Cart

1. What is your spiritual birthday (the day you received new birth in Christ)? Would you share that experience?

2. Have you tried to put the cart before the horse in your Christian walk? Explain.

3. Do you understand that you have been totally forgiven? What can come against your recognition that you are forgiven of all sin (past, present—and future)?

4. Why is it so important to embrace the finality of the cross? (For more on this subject, read the book of Hebrews.)

5. How would you rate yourself as a Christian? Remember that God sees you as a 10. It is time to understand who you are in Christ and acknowledge that truth.

Chapter 5 – Behavior Mod 101

1. Have you or someone you know tried to modify behavior without first receiving identity as a child of God? Explain.

2. Discuss this statement: "Love is the greatest motivator of all." Look at it from God's point of view as well as your own.

3. Think of a difficulty you are facing. Is it a problem or symptom? If it is only a symptom, ask God to help you identify the real problem.

4. Can you relate to the story of the critical boss? Have you ever viewed God in that way? Explain.

5. How does Philippians 4:13 apply to your life?

Chapter 6 – Enemy Territory

1. How has the enemy tried to defeat you in your Christian walk?

2. What tools can you use to overcome the enemy in your life?

3. Have you ever blamed another person for the circumstances you face in life? Explain.

4. Are you still holding bitterness toward a person who has hurt you? If so, pray that God will help you to forgive that person and let go of that offense.

5. Discuss this statement: "God has provided an answer to every problem in His Word." Do you believe this is true? Can you give an example from your own life experience?

Chapter 7 – Victory

1. In your Christian walk, have you focused more on "doing" than on "being"? How has this worked for you?

2. Why do believers love God? Why do you love God?

3. As a whole, have you experienced Christians condemning others or calling them into their righteousness? Which method is more effective long-term?

4. How can Christians better witness to the lost?

5. Have you experienced the "hamster wheel" that was discussed in this chapter? How can someone get off of the wheel?

Chapter 8 – Sinful Nature

1. Read 1 John 2:2. Can you think of someone who needs to hear this verse? If so, pray for an opportunity to share it with him or her.

2. Look in the mirror and tell yourself that you are the righteousness of God in Christ. Keep telling yourself this until it becomes easy to say and you truly believe it.

3. An object's value is often determined by the price paid for it. Think about the price paid for you. How does this truth affect the way you see your value as a person?

4. Why do you think that so many Christians are still so consumed with sin?

5. Read 2 Corinthians 5:11–21. What is the ministry of reconciliation that Christians have been given?

Chapter 9 – Rules and Regulations

1. Do rules and regulations seem to improve people's behavior? Explain.

2. What was the purpose of the Law?

3. What is the greatest commandment? How can believers fulfill it?

4. Read Romans 7:5. How does the Law stir up sin?

5. What is the danger of mixing law and grace? (For a better understanding of mixing law and grace, read the book of Galatians.)

Chapter 10 – True Freedom

1. In your own words, define freedom.

2. Why is the sinner/saint issue so important?

3. How would you describe yourself? Sinner or saint? Does that line up with God's Word or with your feelings?

4. How would you describe the great exchange in your own words?

5. Read John 8:36. What does having freedom in Christ mean to you?

Chapter 11 – Reflections

1. Has the way in which you see yourself changed since you have read this book? If so, how?

2. What are some of the ways the world tries to rehabilitate people? Are these methods effective? Why or why not?

3. Read John 10:10. What does this verse mean to you?

4. Do you base your relationship with Christ more on your performance or His performance on your behalf? Explain.

5. What does your name mean? What is the new name that God has given you?

Thank you for reading this book and for taking the time to go through the discussion questions. I pray that it has been a blessing and that it has helped you on your journey of faith with Jesus. God bless you.